FROM MAN

Memoirs of a Depression Child

ISBN-13 978-1-60145-162-0
ISBN-10 1-60145-162-8

Printed in the United States of America.

Booklocker.com, Inc.
2007

FROM MANURE TO MAHOGANY

Memoirs of a Depression Child

LeRoy Bondy

Contents

Introduction

This is the story of a semi-orphaned waif who caught the brass ring of the American dream to succeed with improbable odds. It is being written because many friends and relatives thought my story would be of interest to others as well. Tom Brokaw wrote an impelling book called "The Greatest Generation" covering the exploits of my generation and he provided short biographies of many outstanding people who had similar backgrounds and met many challenges in their lives. Although mine may not be so unique a story, I have decided to memorialize my path in life for my family, friends and posterity.

Being from a third generation of Norwegian and Dutch immigrants and born into the era of the Great Depression, I miraculously survived a family divorce, was shuttled between relatives during my childhood years (like an orphan), returned from military service in WWII unscathed, completed rigorous engineering training at a mid-West university, returned to military service during the Korean Conflict and subsequently began a career in the business world with many notable achievements. I was married, raised a family, pursued a favorite hobby, traveled extensively in the USA as well as Europe and overall had an interesting and satisfying life. Surely, God had plans for me.

This book is arranged in chapters that reflect the major and distinct events in my life and at the end of each chapter a photo gallery depicts the persons representative of that chapter.

Chapter 1- My Immigrant Connection

"Give me your tired and your poor….."

My Paternal Grandfather and Grandmother were immigrants from Norway who settled in Minnesota where the weather was a milder version of their home country and opportunities were much greater. My Grandfather's name was Knute Wilhelm Bonde, later renamed by Ellis Island as Kvnute W. Bondy.

Grandfather was born in 1844 in Valders, Norway and emigrated alone to Wisconsin at age eighteen. He lived with family friends until he was 22 years of age and then moved to Rice County in Minnesota. He was employed by O. Osmundson at Nerstrand. While working there he met my future Grandmother, Anna Gurine Osmundson.

My Grandmother, Anna Gurine Osmundson, was born in 1850 and her family had emigrated to Minnesota to live with her Uncle, O. Osmundson, in 1854.

They married in 1869 and departed to homestead 160 acres in another township. They traveled by ox-team along with a herd of cattle, had to ferry his oxen & cattle across the river at Fort Snelling. Some of their cattle were stolen by renegade Indians during this event. Their new homestead was completely covered by timber and they spent several months in a nearby neighbor's log cabin while they cleared the land and built their own home. Subsequently, the farm was sold to a son-in-law and my Grandfather purchased a 240 acre farm near the village of Battle Lake, Minnesota. He remained at this second site until his death in 1908. I remember as a youngster traveling from Battle Lake to

Grandfather's farm in a one-horse open sleigh with heated bricks and blankets to stay warm in mid-winter. My Grandfather had died 17-years before I was born so I had no memory of him however the family had a photo of him which reminded me of one of the Smith Brothers of cough drop fame. My Grandmother was still alive when we visited their farm in 1932 but she was bedridden and I remember how tiny she was. She gave me a warm hug but that was our only interface – she died in 1934 when I was 9-years old.

Grandfather became a prosperous farmer and was very active in local politics. He served in the Minnesota Legislature from 1902-1905. In addition he served two terms as President of the Battle Lake Wheat Association, was a Director of the Sverdrup Insurance Company, served as a deputy sheriff and was also an organizer of the Trefoldighed Lutheran Church.

They had nine surviving children named as follows and in chronological birth order:

Caroline Bondy
Wilhelmina Bondy
Ellen Bondy
Wilhelm Bondy
Konow Bondy
Alfred Bondy
Sophie Bondy
Iver Bondy
Melvin Bondy

Certainly, this was a time when big families were required to operate large farms and this was typical of that era. It was also a time when immigrants were willing to take the risks of leaving their familiar homelands to create a successful life without guarantees.

My Father, Melvin Andrew Bondy, was born in 1890 and he was the youngest sibling. He, along with his brothers and sisters, attended the Park Region Lutheran College. Unfortunately, his Father died in 1908 when he was 18 years old and he lost the financial support necessary to complete his college education. My Father then moved to Roland, Minnesota and worked as their Postmaster and did clerical work in a store owned by his Sister Caroline's family. He later obtained a position as bookkeeper at the Battle Lake Minnesota Sanitarium and met my future Mother, Adeline Huyber, who was a Nurse at the Sanitarium. They were married in 1923.

My Maternal Grandparents, Bernard Huyber and Emma Jacobs, emigrated from Holland to Minnesota and were married around the year 1895. They had four children and my mother, Adeline, was next to the youngest. My Grandfather & Grandmother lived in a cabin on the outskirts of Seattle. I have only one recollection of visiting their home but vividly remember Grandfather taking my Brother, Roger, out on the back porch and performing some kind of a rite under a full-moon to cure his warts. When it became my turn I fought vigorously to avoid the same fate and he finally gave up on me. Grandfather Huyber was born in 1876 and died in 1936. Grandmother Huyber was born in 1877 and died in 1949.

I was born in 1925 at Stillwater, Minnesota, baptized in the Lutheran Church with the name, LeRoy Allan Bondy. My only Brother, Roger, was born in 1920 and my only Sister was born in 1928. The following treatise reflects my life's path from birth through final retirement in 2005.

Following are some of the historical events of note that occurred around the time of my birth that affected the U.S. population at large:

In 1920, Woodrow Wilson was defeated for re-election as President and was replaced by Warren G. Harding in 1921. President Wilson used American troops to help defeat German forces in WWI and he proposed that the world leaders establish a "League of Nations" to prevent future major wars. Unfortunately, neither our European allies nor the U.S. public supported President Wilson's ideas and he was defeated. President Harding was beset by corruption & scandel in his administration and in 1923 he died in office of a heart attack.

His successor, Calvin Coolidge, who's motto was "The Business of Government is Business". This seemed appropriate since only private business created jobs and thereby provided taxes to support the government. Consequently, industrial business boomed providing many well paying jobs to urban populations and the stock market exploded. Unfortunately, the rural farming communities never fully recovered from the down-turn in 1920-1921 and families were hard pressed to gain a foothold in the new economy which affected my family as well. Meanwhile, the urban workers were enamored with the prospects of getting rich quick by investing in the stock market and they also were permitted to buy shares on margin (10% down and the balance paid as prices continued to climb).

This was an era of super chain stores (eg; A&P, Woolworth, J.C. Penney, etc.) all providing low down payment installment purchase options for the new automobile, radio, refrigerator, washing machine, etc. This resulted in huge debts for consumers.

This was also the era of super-stars such as Charles Lindbergh, Babe Ruth, Jack Dempsey, Rudolph Valentino, Al Jolson, etc. Less savory super-stars were Al Capone, Bugs Moran, etc.

Commercial airlines started during this era with the Ford Tri-Motor taking the lead in aircraft production and the Federal Highway Act of 1921 started construction of some 50,000 miles of paved highways by the year of my birth, 1925, which spurred automobile sales.

Alas, the lack of government controls of margin buying permitted this trend to continue with wild abandon which created overvalued stocks (today called a "bubble"). In 1929, the bubble burst, stock prices plummeted and brokers demanded that margin buyers pay up immediately. The result was catastrophic, in one month stock prices dropped 40% which, in turn, triggered the great depression and soup lines.

The urban area economic collapse and the ongoing poor economic conditions in the rural areas only aggravated their already marginal living conditions. Thus began the great migration of farmers and agrarian tenants to the Western U.S. where there seemed to be hope for a better life. Although the "grass looked greener on the other side of the fence", reality soon proved otherwise.

Grandfather – Knute W. Bondy – Photo

from his campaign poster.

Circa - 1885

Below, Grandmother – Anna Gurine Bondy (center front) – included in back row

left to right Uncle Iver, Aunt Sophie, Dad & Uncle Fred – others in front row,

left Aunt Ellen and right Aunt Caroline - Circa 1920

Above, Grandmother & Daughter Ellen Bondy at Family Farm – Circa 1910

Below, Grandmother (Front Center) with children & grandchildren – Circa 1926

Grandmother & Grandfather Huyber with Mom above left and her sister Mabel above right.

Mom's brother Marvin center – Circa 1915

Mom left with their dog, Marvin and Mabel – Circa 1910

Chapter 2 - The Family Separation

"Marriage is a many splendored thing but fraught with many perils"

My Father had some formal education in the mercantile accounting business and was able to find some clerical work but with minimal pay or opportunity. This was the beginning of the Great Depression and finding employment was becoming a big problem. When I was two years old, my Maternal Grandparents heard about the wonderful job opportunities in the States of Oregon and Washington and convinced my own parents to move with them to these lands of opportunity. A mini caravan of two automobiles was assembled with my Father and his family driving in a Model T Ford, and my Grandparents with a Son, Marvin, who was 20-years old and a mechanic driving in a Star Touring Car.

Since I was only two years old, my Brother's recollection is as follows. They departed on Good Friday although they were warned that the weather in the Rockies would not be good when they arrived at this time of the year.The trip through the Rocky Mountains was quite adventurous with snow, slick- roads and a few mishaps. When conditions were really bad, Marvin would become the designated driver moving one car up the road a ways then returning to move the other vehicle to the same position. The Model T had bench seats without seat belts in those days and when the car went around steep curves my Mother would slide into my Father on the drivers side which caused some temper tantrums. On one occasion, they were leaving a campground going up a short grade when my Father lost control of the Ford and it rolled backwards smashing into a fence post resulting in a shattered rear window. Nonetheless, we all arrived in Bend, Oregon safe and sound. Shortly thereafter I had a younger sister, Phyllis, who was born after we reached Oregon.

The family settled in to take advantage of the demand for workers in the logging industry. Unfortunately, the work opportunities did not pan out and within a year the entire family moved to Bremerton, Washington to seek other employment near the Navy Yard. Fortunately, my Mother was a Nurse with good job opportunities and my Father found employment in a local retail store. Since my Father and automobiles never reconciled, I remember when he asked my Brother and me to help him push his Model T Ford to a neighbors house which he traded for a Philco radio. We proudly carried this wonderful instrument home to enjoy the sounds of the world. Unfortunately, the stress of nomadic living, the typical incompatibility as well as limited finances created dissension in the family and my parents were divorced when I was eight years old, in 1933. The judge let each of us children decide which parent we preferred to live with and I, alone, chose my Father. I had mixed emotions about the decision but when I saw him crying and seeming so lonely I walked over to his side. The family was physically separated then until I was in college although my Brother would write to me on occasion. We exchanged some photos so he could see what happened in the wild West.

Thus began a series of more nomadic adventures beginning with an immediate move back to Minnesota where we visited with relatives near Battle Lake including my ailing Grandmother and my Uncle Fred who had a local real estate business. My Uncle Fred had a Son, Gordon, who was then in high school and he demonstrated a crystal radio which was a school science project. This was my first exposure to science and it made a deep impression on me. We moved shortly to Roland, Minnesota where I lived with my Aunt Caroline's Son, Knute Rolandson & his wife, Inga, for a period of about four years and my Father worked again in their family store. Knute and Inga had a daughter and two sons younger than I.

I recall attending a one-room schoolhouse about a mile away and many times trudging through deep snow to and from the school with my two younger cousins, Arlo and Kenneth. The path to school was through a heavily wooded area and when it snowed heavily visibility was nil. On one of these bad snow days their was a difference of opinion between my Father and my cousin's parents over the advisability of trying to reach the schoolhouse in this weather. My Father thought I was old enough to make it and off I went along the wooded path but when I arrived at the school house it was closed, so I headed back home. In the meantime my Father became very concerned about his decision and headed out to find me. We met about halfway home and it was a mutually joyous reunion.

My Uncle, Andrew Rolandson (Aunt Caroline's husband) had a large farm nearby with horses, milk cows and sheep. They also had several children. I can remember visiting the farmhouse and their German maid would grab me by the ear and order me to gather firewood. Everyone had duties to perform from the youngest to the oldest and the farm was run like a military establishment. I was drafted on occasion to fulfill various tasks. On occasion, all the boys had to have haircuts and the drill was that the oldest was trimmed by his father and then he had to trim the younger ones in order of age. The tool of choice was the shear used to remove sheep's wool and a mixing bowl was placed on top of each head as a template to achieve matching haircuts.

My two cousins and I were the youngest of the tribe so we had some free time to fool around. On one occasion we were teasing a bull in one of the pastures, being chased by the bull and having to jointly leap over the nearest barb-wire fence to escape. Parental supervision was minimal and longevity was based upon the survival of the fittest.

When I was about twelve years old, in 1937, my Father heard from his Brother in Richland, Montana that there were good paying jobs because of the Fort Peck Dam project so we were soon on a train to Montana. I was now in the sixth grade of school with a lot of handy work experience from the Rolandson farm.

Who knows how events can change personalities and trigger irreconciable differences between spouses. It terminated my parents marriage in 1933 even though it started with good intentions and great hopes for the future. Although it separated the family siblings for a long period of time, we have now renewed our former relationships and all is well. I must thank the entire Bondy clan for taking me in as one of their own and allowing me to mavture in a somewhat normal fashion.

My Sister Phyllis and I – Circa 1931

My Father – Circa 1910

Mom, Sister Phyllis & Brother Roger – Circa 1980

Knute Rolandson operated Roland Store northeast of Oklee until moving into Oklee to go into the farm implement business.

Above, My Father in front of Roland Store with Knute Rolandson home next and Rolandson farm beyond.

Below, Family of Uncle Andrew Rolandson & Aunt Caroline in front center – Knute far left in back row.

Chapter 3 - The Cowboy Years

"These were the best of times and the worst of times"

My Father's brother had a large ranch outside of Richland, Montana and I ended up living with them while my Father took a job in town at a local bar & restaurant owned by a nephew. My Uncle, Knute Konow Bondy (known as K.K. Bondy), was a homesteader with a ranch of some one thousand acres which contained a herd of milk cows, a lot of chickens, some turkeys, some horses and several large cultivated fields of wheat. My uncle and his wife, Emma, had thirteen children (twelve when I arrived) and they lived in a small ranch house with no electricity, a neraby bunkhouse and an outdoor toilet (out house). There were seven boys (with one set of twins) and six girls with many of them grown, married and employed elsewhere. All of the remaining boys (5) slept in the bunkhouse and the girls slept in the house (somewhere).

We were only allowed in the house to eat and occasionally, after school, to listen to a battery-operated radio, which provided shows like Jack Armstrong & Orphan Annie. My Uncle was a short, overweight man with a bald head and he would sit close to his radio with his head in his hands listening intently to the programs. In those days of early radio, it required two external batteries – one a 6-volt wet-cell car battery to provide power to the vacuum-tube filaments and a series of dry-cell batteries to provide the operating voltages for the vacuum-tube amplifiers. In addition, a long outdoor antenna was required to obtain decent reception.

I can recall a story about my paternal Grandmother chastising my

Uncle K.K. for having so many children. To which he responded, "The Bible says we are to multiply and inherit the earth". My Grandmothers retort was, "Yes, but he did not intend for you to do it all by yourself".

I was the youngest of the boys and my twin cousins were about a year older than I. The routine on the farm, and any farm for that matter, was to distribute the daily chores proportional to the age of the children. My chores were to get dressed early in the morning, saddle my horse, find the cows out on the range and bring them into the barn for milking. Then I would go into the main house for breakfast and immediately thereafter go to the barn and milk the cows assigned to me. If it were Winter with school in session, my cousins and I would saddle up our respective horses after chores and leave for our one-room schoolhouse - about ten miles away. The school had about fifteen students. We would leave the horses at a neighboring farm for pick up after school. Since boys will be boys, we would occasionally race each other on the way home to the chagrin of Uncle K.K. who insisted we not overheat the horses – he would feel their necks for signs of sweating to determine if we were behaving.

Schooling was something I was really into, and I looked forward to whatever I could glean from the various teachers in session. Almost every year we had a different teacher, usually a student teacher from one of the nearby towns. My favorite teacher came from California, he reminded me of Ichabod Crane and was very well educated with a classical music background. Between classes he would play classical music on his violin which was quite a break from our normal fare of cowboy & barn-dance music.

During classes, I particularly enjoyed the fact that all grade levels were in the same room, usually two or three students in each grade level, and we were permitted to participate in the higher grade subjects if we felt competent. I began in the sixth grade at this school and since math was one of my favorite subjects, I was able to participate at the seventh and eighth grade levels. In addition, I learned a lot about farming and could name every breed of cow, horse, chicken and pig as well as the value of crop-rotation, obviously this training was geared toward a farming career which I assumed would be my role in life.

We even had sports to some extent, weather permitting, primarily a baseball team consisting of seven boys (since that was all the boys there were in the school) and some well worn equipment (as I recall, one baseball, three well worn gloves and one bat). We had a good time practicing this sport and once we played against a City of Richland team but sustained a terrible loss (they insisted on using nine players).

During the Spring season, the workload increased tremendously with wheat planting and the associated preparation of the fields. This included moving large amounts of manure mixed with straw that had accumulated in the barn over the Winter months onto the fields as pre-planting fertilizer which would be worked into the soil by a tractor drawn harrow. The manure spreading was accomplished by using a horse-drawn sled (no wheels) piled high by pitchfork with manure and subsequently hauled to the site to be spread evenly by pitchfork over the field.

In late Fall, the manure that had accumulated over the Summer months was removed and used to bank the lower extremities of the main house and bunk house for insulation during the coming Winter months. The composting that occurred helped to warm the buildings. Of course, in the Spring it was all removed and spread on the fields. It seemed manure was the most important product on the farm! Usually a good bit was deposited on our shoes and clothing but no one seemed to mind since we all shared the same fragrance.

In the early Summer months, one of my main duties was to saddle my horse and patrol the fields to keep unwanted animals from partaking of the succulent crops. I would occasionally stray from my post to chase herds of wild horses, just to see if I could keep up and even unlimbered my lasso a few times hoping to catch me a horse. Luckily, I was never successful or I probably would never have been around for this autobiography. It seemed we had only one successful crop of wheat every other year with a series of catastrophes that destroyed the wheat fields including locusts, drought or a multitude of green cut-worms. One year the sky would be blackened by millions of locusts that swarmed over the succulent, growing wheat fields devouring everything in their path. Another year, the entire ground would be covered with cut-worms appearing like a continuous green sheet moving slowly through the growing fields eating every thing in their path. When we walked through the fields the worms squished underfoot and they would climb up our pant-legs. In another year, the rains would cease and the crops dried out completely, leaving nothing but stubble. No harvesting and minimal income in these years.

Towards the end of the Summer season, we had a cattle round-up to brand all of the new calves and assure they did not end up on some other farm. The brand was a copyright of bovine property. At the same time, some of the young stallions were castrated to assure they could be trained as workhorses or saddle horses. The bull calves were also castrated to prevent unruly activities and produce good beef stock. Definitely not one of my favorite duties. Also, this was a time to slaughter and butcher certain pigs, cattle and chickens for the preparation of the meals required for the pending harvest crews. Fertile cows were inseminated by bulls provided by neighboring farmers which insulated our farm life from unruly bulls in the herd.

Firearms were commonplace on the local ranches - they ranged from twelve gage shotguns todeer rifles and we had a few always at the ready for prowling coyotes and wolves. I didn't have my own gun, but saw an advertisement in a magazine for salesmen to sell cure-all salves with the grand prize of a 22-caliber rifle. I decided I could do that and proceeded to sell salves to all of our neighbors resulting in the prized rifle. About the only thing you could kill with this weapon were prairie-dogs, so this became my game of choice, and to encourage me my oldest cousin, Kenneth, paid me a penny for every tail I produced. After a hard days hunting. I didn't get rich, but became an important exterminator for the farm.

Kenneth was an auto mechanic and also owned the bar & restaurant where my Father worked in Richland. Kenneth would come to the ranch periodically to help with vehicle repairs. On one occasion he mounted an automobile generator on top of a pole with a windmill blade attached that would operate a yard light when the wind blew hard enough (the bulb was a 6-volt auto headlamp). This was about as high-tech as it got on the ranch.

As I recollect, it was just before the cattle branding season and we were visited by a very agitated neighboring farmer. He claimed there was a cattle rustler in the area stealing unbranded calves from the grazing fields and he knew which way the thief was headed with his contraband. This spurred a reaction from my older cousins who allowed as how we should immediately form a posse and pursue this rustler. My cousins and some local ranchers proceeded to saddle up their horses and retrieve their rifles with the intention of leaving post haste. When I caught wind of the proposed action, I immediately saddled my horse and with my trusty 22-caliber rifle I joined the posse. My involvement was short lived when I was informed that this venture did not include children and off they went without me. I cannot remember the outcome of this incident, but later heard that a sheriff was called to also participate in the search.

During the harvesting period, hired crews moved from farm to farm with large combines pulled by large steam-driven tractors that would cut and thresh the wheat in one operation. Dump trucks would follow the combine and fill up with wheat flowing out of a trough on the combine. When one truck was full another would take its place and the harvest continued from morning to night. The wheat was transported to silos in the nearby town of Richland and when the silos overflowed the wheat was dumped in piles nearby. Eventually, the wheat was sold and loaded onto rail cars for distribution throughout the country. I can only remember one year when the wheat production exceeded demand and of course the price dropped accordingly. The wheat stubble was cut and stored in a large pile behind the barn (straw) and used to cover the layers of fresh cow manure that accumulated in the barn. A sanitation procedure between milking sessions.

On rare occasions we would venture into the big city of Richland (population 2,500) and visit the county fair or partake of real restaurant food. Richland was the anchor town for the local farming communities and provided the silos for crop storage and subsequent rail shipments as well as the sales & service of farm equipment. My Father had given me a dollar (a tidy sum in those days) to spend at the fair. I can remember getting carried away with too much soda-pop plus ice cream at the county fair and subsequently up-chucking most of it in an alley. On the ranch, we were used to only plain meat and potatoes.

Between planting and harvest, we would visit some of the neighboring farmers for food and conversation. I can remember on one visit when we were seated at a neighbor's large dining table with approximately twelve diners and being visited during the meal by various livestock, including pigs and chickens. Doors were designed to be left open for fresh air and the roaming livestock decided to join us for dinner. No one seemed to mind.

When I reached age fourteen, my Uncle K.K. informed me that this was the age when everyone had to learn to drive. Our main method of transportation and hauling was an old International truck which had been selected as my learning vehicle. We were on our way to visit one of our neighboring farmers for Sunday dinner and they put me behind the wheel for the short trip. Unfortunately, the truck was big and I was small in stature so I had to stand to see out the windshield. So far so good, but as we turned into our neighbors driveway I missed the brake pedal and took out their clothes-line poles which became a long term family joke. Our other mode of transportaion was a Model-A Ford which my Aunt Emma re-upholstered with some striped awning material she picked up in Richland and we were the center of attention.when we appeared in town.

Although we had no electricity, running water or plumbing, I don't remember anyone complaining about our misfortune. In fact, all our neighbors were in the same boat and this was a normal way of life. The boys bunkhouse was a one room affair with two double beds that accommodated four to five of us at various times. There was one pot-bellied stove that used cow-pies (dried manure) for fuel and in the Winter it would die out sometime in the night. We awoke with frost on the bedding from our breath and jumped quickly into our overalls which were usually stiff from the frozen moisture and required some vigorous leg movements before proceeding with the necessary early morning chores. During the night we would hear Coyotes yipping outside our only window with our dog barking and anxious to pursue the critters. Conventional wisdom said that any pursuing dogs would be ambushed by the rest of the pack and killed so we kept the dog inside. Our only light after dark was a kerosene lamp by which we could tell stories, play various musical instruments and rough-house until bedtime.

Two of my older cousins were excellent musicians even though they never had formal lessons and cowboy music was the norm. As a little aside, one of the neighbors operated a large sheep ranch and when the ewes delivered their small lambs if there were more than one born to a mother she would select only one to nurse since she was only capable of sustaining one lamb. This resulted in a small percentage of "bum lambs" or lambs that were not permitted to suckle and would eventually die. The rancher offered these bum lambs free to anyone who would take them and care for them which included bottle feeding and keeping them warm. As a reward, he offered to buy them back if they survived to adulthood. My twin cousins and I each took a bum lamb to care for and provided the bottle feeding as well as keeping them warm near my aunt's wood burning stove. The lambs all survived and grew into frisky adults which we ultimately sold back to the rancher. I used my earnings to buy an Hawaiian guitar and spent hours trying to learn how to play music on the instrument to no avail. One day an older cousin visited, picked up my guitar and proceeded to play several country western tunes which completely amazed me. As a result, I gave him my guitar and decided music was not my forte.

Bathing in the Winter was a real exercise in logistics, with one large laundry tub filled with hot water (carried from the main house). The order of bathing was oldest first and youngest last. Since I was the youngest, the bath water was luke-warm and somewhat dirty for my turn. Luckily, baths were infrequent and only in the Winter with the potbellied stove red hot. Warm weather bathing was by improvised outdoor showers - an empty metal barrel with holes punched in the bottom, suspended on a wooden tripod and filled with hot water. Otherwise a dip in the nearby river.

When I was in the eighth grade at our one-room schoolhouse, our teacher for the year was from the town of Richland and at the end of the school year she convinced my Father that I should make arrangements to attend high school in the Fall since my abilities were commensurate with the academic requirements. This would necessitate passing a written examination prior to acceptance and she volunteered to provide the necessary coaching. All went well and I was accepted at a high school in, Peerless, Montana a small town of a few hundred residents. This required lodging in a nearby boarding facility. To subsidize the cost, my Uncle would bring a butchered pig or cow on a monthly basis. Generally, I visited the farm each month and was delivered back to high school on a following Sunday. This was a very exciting time in my life with segregated classes, a library and extracurricular sports - this was really living. At the boarding facility, I had one room partitioned with plywood and just big enough for a single bed and a study area. We had a common outdoor toilet and one wash bowl to keep tidy hands. There was a common dining room that served three meals a day and I don't recall whether the food was good or bad - whatever, we survived to study another day.

Uncle K.K. & Aunt Emma, back row far left & far right – Circa 1925
Twelve of thirteen children shown – Cousin Gerald held by his Father

Aunt Emma Bondy, front center and all thirteen children – Circa 1975

Cousin Gerald, back row third from right

Chapter 4 - Back to Minnesota

"Thank God for caring relatives"

I had just finished my tenth grade at the Peerless, Montana high school when my Father advised me we were moving back to Minnesota to live with one of his other brothers, Iver Bondy, in Bemidji, Minnesota. To me, Bemidji was a big city with about five thousand residents, had a downtown section and was the home of the famous statue of Paul Bunyon with his Big Blue Ox. My uncle lived on the outskirts of the city about two miles from downtown. He had no indoor plumbing but he had electric lights which to me was amazing technology. I was welcomed with open arms by my Uncle, his wife, Minnie and daughter, Laverne (who was a year older than I) and became a part of their family. Laverne (Vernie) and I had great times together – like a brother and a sister. We had great fun playing pranks on unsuspecting out-of –town college students who stayed in nearby cabins during the school terms. I recall on one occasion a young lad in his second year at Bemidji State Teachers College was dropped off by his parents in one of the cabins. We knew him quite well since the cabins were in close proximity to my Uncle's home. Prior to this particular drop off, Vernie and I stuffed one her stockings with paper and fitted one of her shoes onto the foot then we climbed in a window of his cabin, arranged the pillows to look like a body and let the false leg protrude from the covers. Needless to say there was great commotion when the parents opened the door while Vernie and I were hiding behind a tree laughing ourselves silly. It turns out this particular boy joned the Navy submarine fleet about the same time I joined the regular Navy and we met again briefly in

Hawaii while I was on my way to board the USS Cleveland. We never made contact after that time.

Bemidji had banks, churches, parks, a large lake, a library, a hospital, a modern school and public transportation - anything you might desire, at least for me. During the Summer months, a grandstand at the public park would provide band music and other events - I remember when the Joe Louis-Max Smelling fight was broadcast over the park speaker system which drew a large crowd. There was even a country club for the golf enthusiasts and I worked for a while as a caddy to earn some extra money - enough to buy a real Kodak camera. My first introduction to modern medicine was undergoing a tonsilectomy at a local doctor's office and since we lived on the outskirts of Bemidji, my cousin Vernie and I caught the bus downtown (the fare was 5-cents) where my tonsils were removed and we immediately caught the bus back home – post operative treatment was ice cream.

Although most of the Bondy clan were Lutherans, my Aunt & Uncle were Seventh Day Adventists with very strict dietary and social rules. The rules also applied to me since I was a permanent boarder and I was a frequent visitor to their local church on Saturdays. Nonetheless, I obtained a job at the main Lutheran Church as a broadcast technician and interfaced with the local radio station for the regular Sunday broadcasts. It was too early in my life to establish an independent spiritual awareness so I followed whatever the local requirements dictated (when in Rome, do as the Romans do).

During my first year in Bemidji, I managed to earn five dollars and bought a used bike that required significant repairs so I became a frequent visitor to the local bicycle shop. Since I had to make most of the repairs myself this was an important learning experience for me and confirmed my interest in technical pursuits. With my own bicycle, I was able to tour the city at will and visit my most important destination, the city library. The library gave me access to technical publications that peaked my interest in science. Those were the days.

Since I was a new kid on the block, it took several months to find friends with similar interests; however, I soon joined a close knit group of boys and girls with whom to commiserate. We traveled together (locally), played sports together, rode our bikes together and got into mischief together.

Lake Bemidji was one of the larger lakes in Minnesota and attracted a lot of tourists during the Summer season. A large fleet of motor boats plied the water and I had a few turns at the helm thanks to certain relatives. Canoes and oar-boats were also common craft on the lake. There was a city recreation area that accommodated both swimmers and boats. This was a favorite hang-out for me and my friends.

Bemidji was known as the ice-box of the nation with winter temperatures hovering in a range from 20 degrees below zero to as low as 50 degrees below zero. At the extremes, automobiles wouldn't start and only buses and pedestrians moved. We learned to dress appropriately for the cold weather and I cannot remember being affected negatively by the experience.

My Uncle had a fish house on the lake which was similar to an outdoor toilet, painted black inside, with a small kerosene stove and a large hole sawed through the ice. I would spend days at a time spear-fishing for Pike and other lake fish - this required the use of homemade decoys that we constantly moved about to attract hungry fish. When a large fish appeared it would stop to examine the decoy and then quickl;y strike which gave a fisherman about five seconds to thrust the spear into the fish. Needlessly to say, there were more misses than strikes but I did manage to bring home eight to ten pound fish on occasion - I have a photo somewhere with one of my prize trophies.

A booming industry in the Winter period were ice houses that sawed out large blocks of ice which were transported to warehouses and then covered with sawdust to insulate them from warm weather. In the Summer months, ice was delivered to homes for use in their ice-boxes (few if any refrigerators existed then). During the Summer months we would chase the ice delivery trucks to snatch chunks of loose ice as a cooling treat.

My high school days were interesting and fruitful with exposure to mathematics, science and other academic subjects. Again, I was stimulated to explore technology whenever the opportunity presented itself. The Government had established small electronic clubs which were akin to the popular ham-radio clubs and I joined to learn as much as I could about the world of electronics. Apparently, the Government was planning ahead for a pending military conflict. In any event I excelled in the mathematics and science curriculum which was to serve me well in the near future. Since I was somewhat shy and unaccustomed to city culture, I made only a few long standing friends during my Junior and Senior years.

Chapter 5 - World War II

"On December 7th, 1941 a date that will live in infamy.........."

During my Junior year in Bemidji high school we were somewhat aware of the war raging in Europe but it seemed remote and not really affecting our life. Then Pearl Harbor was attacked by the Japanese and every boy I knew was ready to sign up and fight the enemy. We were all afraid the war would be over before we would be old enough to enlist. When I finally graduated in the Spring of 1943, I hightailed it to the Navy Recruiting Office intending to enlist for the duration but was turned down due to poor eyesight. Not to be deterred, I went to the library and checked out a book "The Bates Method of Improving your Eyesight". After a few weeks of this exercise program, I again visited the Navy Recruiting Office but much to my chagrin my eyesight had not improved. Since the Navy was my service of choice, I continued the eye exercise program and for the third time I was again rejected by the recruiting office. By this time the Summer was over and I had received my draft notice and was required to report to Fort Snelling (Minneapolis) within thirty days. I figured I was in the Army now and not behind the plough.

As the time approached for me and some of my friends to board the bus for Fort Snelling, I suggested to my friends that I take them horse-back riding at a local stable as a last get together. It was agreed that four of us would partake of the adventure and since I was an experienced horseman I would lead the group. When we arrived, the stable had a variety of horses from frisky to the laid back. I chose the frisky horse and recommended that my friends choose the more laid back. We proceeded slowly along the riding trail which meandered through the local forest and after a few minutes I suggested we get it in gear and move the horses to a trot and then a gallop. My steed was much faster and soon I had left the rest far behind but when making a sharp turn in the trail my horse slipped and fell with me still in the saddle. The horn of the saddle saved me from being crushed under the weight of the horse and I was able to extricate myself with no problem. When the other members caught up, I was dusting myself off and had the horse on his feet again so we completed our ride albeit in a more conservative manner. A good time was had by all and we parted with the intention of meeting early Monday morning for our bus ride to Minneapolis.

The night after our riding adventure, I awoke with sharp abdominal pains and my Aunt called our local doctor who diagnosed me with appendicitis. Subsequently, I was taken to the local hospital and underwent an appendectomy that same night. Monday came and I had not reported for my induction bus ride. That same day the Sheriff arrived looking for an AWOL inductee but was satisfied that my excuse was valid for another thirty days. Finally, I reported to Fort Snelling for my medical examination and took a series of aptitude tests. I was not only accepted as a conscript but due to high marks in my aptitude tests I was offered a choice of attending the Army Officer Candidate school or the US Navy electronic training school. Needless to say, I picked the Navy and in January,1944, I was sent to Farragut, Idaho for basic training which included marching drills, firearm familiarity, identiifcation drills for enemy ships and aircraft, swimming and high-dive abandon ship drills. The swimming pool was housed in a large Quonset Hut facility with minimal insulation from the Winter weather and snow would sift into the swimming pool area. To keep us healthy we were given sulpha pills each morning and, of course, we had every immune shot known to man.

After basic training, I was sent to their primary electronic training school in Great Lakes (Chicago) for an intensive three month introduction to electronic theory. After successful completion, I was sent to their advanced training facility in Monterey, California for another three months of training in Sonar and Radar operating theory.

Finally I was transferred to Treaure Island (San Francisco) for another three months of hands-on training in radar maintenance and repair.

After about a year of intensive training, I became an ETR-2 (Electronic Technician Radar) and was sent to the Naval medical center to determine my condition to serve in various Naval operations. Since my eyesight was below the minimums for fleet duty I was in a dilemma about being either a land-lubber or a shipboard sailor. What to do! I decided not to wear my glasses for the pending medical examination and as I stood in line with many others for the eye exam it became clear that there was only one eye chart in use. Consequently, I memorized the response from those ahead of me, was accepted with 20-20 eyesight and assigned for duty aboard the USS Cleveland (Light Cruiser CL-55)) as the sole technician in charge of the maintenance and repair of the ship's new radar installations. I quickly retrieved my eyeglasses and the rest is history, never to be questioned about my vision again.

The Cleveland had recently been upgraded with the latest in both search and fire-control radars which provided long-range interception of enemy targets as well as automatic, computer control of the 5-inch anti-aircraft guns. Unkown to me at the time, the 5-inch shells had proximity fuses as well which permitted near misses to still bring down enemy aircraft. My sole duty on the Cleveland was to keep the radar systems maintained and operation on a 24-7 basis. Since I was on call day and night, guard duties and other maintenance duties were eliminated so I could use my free time as I wished. I had the opportunity to pursue other technical training through correspondence courses.

I joined the USS Cleveland in the Pacific Theatre on or about January 14, 1945 just prior to the campaign to recapture the Phillipines from the Japanese. On February 13th we were involved in the bombardment of Corregidor and on February 16th we witnessed Army paratroopers landing on Corregidor which was shortly under U.S. control. By the end of February, McArthur's forces occupied Manila and we continued to patrol the Phillipine islands. On June 17th we were dispatched to Subic Bay in British North Borneo to protect Australian troops invading this island and assigned to shore battery operations with close-in support. On June 25th we were dispatched to Manila to pick up General Douglas McArthur and return him to Borneo. The USS Cleveland was selected because of its advanced radar systems that could avoid any Japanese naval vessels and the Cruiser's speed made a successful enemy submarine attack unlikely. Upon arrival in Manila, we were granted a day of liberty to visit the City and some R&R. Before we left the ship we were issued condoms which was a new item to me but as we reached the dock we were surrounded by pimps and prostitutes looking for some Yankee dollars. I realized then the rationale behind this Navy issue. Along with a few other naïve buddies we shied away from these questionable temptations and headed for the city proper. Unfortunately, Manila was heavily damaged by the fighting and only a few businesses were operating, with the Red Cross building being the most popular. We were permitted to venture up to the front lines outside the City proper with the mop-up fighting still raging and the scent of decaying bodies overwhelming.

Back to the ship, we were ordered to don our dress whites and stand at attention as General McArthur was piped aboard - naturally, he was late and we were weary from the heat. Finally, he was aboard with his large staff and as a reward for our taxi duty we each received an 8 x 10, signed photo of McArthur. I thought it was very exciting but most of my shipmates were disgusted with the fanfare in the middle of a war and they threw the photos overboard. I kept my copy and hid it under my mattress to avoid any retribution. Nonetheless, we departed Manila on June 27th and delivered McArthur to Borneo where he waded ashore with great fanfare and a bevy of photographers to celebrate another pending victory. We subsequently returned McArthur to Manila and awaited our next assignment.

Our next campaign took us to Okinawa on July 13th with the invasion underway and we were assisting with our substantial firepower. This was also the time of the massive kamikaze attacks by Japanese suicide pilots and our modem fire control radar earned its keep by directing our five inch guns at radar targets with great accuracy. Many ships were struck and damaged but fortunately none of the attacks made it to our cruiser. As the campaign drew to a close, we received word on August 10th that two atomic bombs had been dropped on Japanand they had agreed to an unconditional surrender. Great celebration ensued as the troops on the beach were firing rockets into the air and everyone aboard ship were yelling, laughing and talking.. But just as things settled down, a new wave of suicide pilots arrived and began attacking our fleet sinking the USS Pennsylvania next to us and damaging many others. Needless to say, the Navy assumed the surrender was a trick and ordered all ships out to sea to assess the situation but finally on August 20th the all clear sounded with the attacks apparently only remnants of die hard Japanese military leaders.

On September 9th we were ordered to take positions around the Japanese mainland to assure a peaceful surrender. On the way, we encountered one of the notorious Western Pacific hurricanes that swamped or beached many of the smaller vessels but we managed to slog along with waves over fifty feet high and we bobbed like a cork. I had to go topside to investigate a radar equipment problem and the waves outside looked as high as the Empire State building - needless to say, I had a firm grip on all protuberances as I made my way to safety. After the storm had subsided, we made a bee-line to the Japanese port of Wakayama and dropped anchor on September 15th to asses the situation. Advance invasion parties went ashore and reported there was no visible resistance which resulted in another liberty occasion with visits to the city proper. We encountered very polite citizens although no women were in sight. There was some English spoken by shopkeepers - I visited one of the engineering supply stores and bought a slide rule made from bamboo which was an excellent product albeit with Japanese characters. As the weapons were rounded up by Marine and Army troops they were stockpiled in heaps of contraband with each sailor allowed to collect one as a keepsake trophy - I selected a Japanese rifle complete with bayonet and retained the weapon for about ten years.

Shortly thereafter, on October 28, 1945 we dropped anchor in Tokyo Bay off Yokosuka to provide cover for the USS Missouri and General McArthur's surrender ceremony with Japan and the U.S. allies. The USS Cleveland and its crew had helped to win a war.

Soon we were ordered back to Hawaii for reassignment and as we approached the Islands we were ordered to throw all loose equipment overboard including a lot of valuable items I used in my radar maintenance. This seemed like treason at the time but I later learned that the Government did not want surplus equipment affecting the recovery of our industrial base in the United States. Upon dropping anchor in Hawaii, we were visited by a small supply ship that brought aboard cold, fresh milk which we sailors lapped up like hungry cats. Since I did not have enough battle ribbons and campaign stars, I was not eligible for immediate discharge and was reassigned to a ship operating in the Key West area with similar radar equipment. This was like a vacation in the Tropics with a lot of liberty to enjoy the beaches and other sights nearby. In June, 1946, I was returned to Fort Snelling in Minnesota for honorable discharge. A civilian once again.

Above, my high school graduation picture – Circa 1943

My new recruit picture – Circa 1944

My Cousin Vernie trying on my uniform –

Circa 1945

My Uncle Iver, Aunt Minnie & Vernie –

Circa 1945

My Sister Phyllis & Dad in front of Paul Bunyan-

Uncle Iver in back – Circa 1948

My Cousin Vernie and I with Paul Bunyan & his big blue Ox – Circa 1990

<u>Chapter 6</u> - A Post-war Education

"The mind is a terrible thing to waste"

Although it was a great relief to return to the unregimented civilian life, I had made no concrete plans for the future. I knew I wanted to pursue more technical training, building upon my Navy experience and the G. I. Bill provided the opportunity to investigate the options. But first, I had to complete the obligatory reunions and parties with my service buddies which seemed to never end. One of my non-military friends said there was a boom going on in local Minnesota highway construction and suggested that if we had a dump truck we could cash in on this wonderful opportunity – in addition he was a licensed truck driver and could do most of the work. Since I had saved all of my military pay during the war my entrepreneurial genes kicked in and soon we were in Minneapolis trading in my Hudson Terraplane car and several extra bucks for a shiny, new dump truck. I was now in business (Summer weather only) and proceeded to hire my friend as well as a cousin to provide 24-hour service to the highway contractors. All went well in the beginning until my drivers would get drunk after payday and didn't show for agreed work hours – I was stuck with driving two shifts then which was a downer and most other experienced truck drivers were fully employed. Then maintenance bills started rolling in, particularly tires since the wear and tear was brutal and they were expensive. I stuck it out until early Fall and had enough, so I decided to sell the truck and pursue a more likely career. Unfortunately, this was a bad time of the year to sell dump-trucks with the operating season coming to an end so my instigator friend and I started driving West to find a buyer and after reaching Western North

Dakota I was successful in trading the truck for another car. The return trip home turned into another adventure since I had spent most of my money and my friend had none – we had to siphon gas from parked cars during the night for fuel enough to get home. That ended my business desires for a few years.

Finally, as the Fall school term approached, I enrolled at our local Bemidji State Teachers College with the understanding that full credit would be accepted at the University of Minnesota after one year. As my homework increased, my parties decreased until I became a full-time, dedicated student. Thus, the next four years would be the most rewarding of my life as the former farm-boy learned to become a future white-collar engineer.

Because of my electronics training in the Navy, I was hired by a local appliance store to repair radios that customers would return on a regular basis. It was an interesting job and well within my capabilities – these talents were rare in those days. My relatives couldn't understand why I was planning to move to the University of Minnesota in Minneapolis to study electrical engineering when I already had a good, well paying job near home. I guess they didn't understand the usefulness of a higher education since I was the only one of my extended family of relatives that pursued education beyond high school.

The GI Bill provided a wonderful subsidy to veterans of WWII which paid for tuition & books plus a small living allowance and I urged my veteran friends to consider this opportunity – sadly, none seemed to be interested. During my first year at Bemidji State Teachers college, I continued my job at the appliance store between classes and studied hard at night. The teachers college was rigorous concerning communication skills which served me well in my career – a skill requirement that was unfortunately lacking in the University engineering programs.

The first year went fast and I soon found myself at the University of Minnesota Institute of Technology and ensconced in an all male dormitory with a room mate. This sophomore year emphasized physics, chemistry and mathematics and it became a whirlwind of classes and laboratory along with much homework which convinced some of my classmates to switch to other disciplines. To supplement my veterans allowance I became the dormitory janitor, worked in one of the college cafeterias and joined the Navy Reserve as a week-end warrior once a month. When classes were over in the Summer, I was hired along with some other students to clean and paint all of the dormitory rooms before the next school term.

In my junior year, the electrical engineering subjects were included along with physics, mathematics and the obligatory laboratory sessions. Again, I worked as the dormitory janitor, was employed in the college cafeteria and continued my week-end warrier activities. However, by now I had mastered the routine of classes, study and work with time left over to enjoy some of the extra-curricular activities including inter-mural basketball and some co-educational social functions. As this year ended, I once again began my Summer dormitory maintenance job but also took time to enjoy various social activities. One of these was a dinner-dance on the local river paddle boat and I had a blind date who became my wife after the following year's graduation.

In my senior year, school work became less hectic and I became more involved in after class activties including assisting with the arrangement of various athletic and social events. I was also elected dormitory president and participated in various administration meetings. A notable event was participating in our senior prom arrangements and meeting a budding vocalist, Patti Page, who went on to become a popular singing star. Finally, we spent time preparing resumes that were to be provided to various interested companies looking for new graduates and I was hired by a company in Cleveland, Ohio (ECM) making motor control modules. This was fine since my bride to be lived in Cambridge, Ohio.

I graduated on June 10, 1950 with a degree in electrical engineering, was married on June 25, 1950 and began my new job in Cleveland to enjoy a real paying career as an electrical engineer. Unfortunately, in October, 1950 I was recalled by the Navy during the Korean conflict because of my unique electonic skills. This involved a six week training school for Navy instructors in San Diego.The good news was that they transferred me to Hawaii to teach radar & sonar classes for sea going sailers and I was permitted to bring my wife and my automobile along for the ride.

Life in Hawaii was wonderful and we found apartment accommodations adjacent to Waikaki Beach which is now fully occupied by high-rise hotels. The weather was perfect and there were a lot of sights to see which was easy with our own automobile. I taught two classes each work day and had frequent guard duties at night – not the white collar job I expected but a pleasant living environment.

The duty period was short and in June, 1952 I was again honorably discharged and released in San Diego, California but not before I was offered a commission as an Ensign in the regular Navy if I would commit for three more years which I declined.

Chapter 7 - The Business World

"The business of government is business"

With my Korean Conflict Navy obligations out of the way, I was ready to resume my engineering career. Since I was discharged in San Diego, California with a sick newborn child, my wife and I decided to remain in California and assess the opportunities since we needed income immediately to pay some hefty medical bills. Shortly thereafter, I was employed by the Douglas Aircraft Company in Long Beach, California, to assist in the development of their first jet powered airliner, the DC-8. My initial responsibilities were to assist senior engineers with the design of instrumentation systems necessary to proof test all aspects of the aircraft's construction and performance. This was right up my alley and I became very proficient in this technical area. Within a year, I was promoted to the position of engineering manager of all instrumentation systems and was asked to assist other Douglas facilities with their respective programs. My particular expertise was in testing materials and systems under dynamic conditions which required knowledge of instrumentation bandwidth and optimum sensor application. I was asked to install instrumentation equipment and sensors for Navy aircraft landing gear life testing at the Douglas Naval Aircraft development facility in Santa Monica which lasted for several months and I traveled to other Douglas facilities to support similar testing programs. This was engineering nirvana.

When Douglas Aircraft became jointly involved with Boeing in a top-secret space vehicle program for the military, with the name "Dynasoar", I was selected as part of the advanced development team with the responsibility to travel throughout the United States and evaluate wind tunnels that could test hypersonic vehicles. It also involved attending special classes on the mathematics of ballistic flight. Unfortunately, after about a year on this project it was canceled. The Dynasoar name was an acronym for Dynamic Soaring Vehicle which was to be used as a cold-war weapon delivery system. Interestingly, it was the precursor of the current Space Shuttle which used much of the information gathered for the design of the Dynasoar. The Minute Man missile success negated the need for the Dynasoar vehicle.

I subsequently resumed my normal duties as instrumentation manager and I was involved in many presentations at group meetings which prompted me to form a Douglas Toastmasters Club to polish my contemporaneous speaking skills. We would meet monthly with other clubs in the area to compare and critique our speaking abilities. This was a wonderful experience and would pay off in later years.

As I approached my fourth year at the Douglas Aircraft Company, my department manager resigned his position to accept employment elsewhere. He informed the personnel manager that I was the best candidate to replace him. However, when I was interviewed by the personnel manager he advised me that I was too young for this responsibility and they would be looking outside the company for a replacement. Here I was thirty years old which seemed a mature and responsible age and it deflated my ego. The replacement manager was an older gentleman in his fifties (which seemed old to me) with some technical background but no clue about the instrumentation technology. I continued my role as instrumentation guru and became involved in the design of some new specialized products. One of these was the combination of a multi-turn potentiometer with a constant force angular spring and pulley system that was capable of measuring movements that exceeded tens of feet which was necessary to measure wing-tip deflections on the DC-8 aircraft during maximum wing loading stress tests. The device became known as a "String Pot" and now supports annual private business sales volumes in excess of $50M. Since the development of this product was performed using government funds, the technology became public-owned and could not be patented. The major company manufacturing this product now is Celesco located in Southern California.

During this same period, I had become involved with a unique inductive position sensor known as an LVDT (Linear Variable Differential Transformer) manufactured by only two companies at that time. It was an indestructible product for measuring dimensional movement in our aircraft test programs and I purchased many of them from the major supplier, Schaevitz Engineering in Pennsauken, New Jersey. I was also aware that military aircraft designers were looking for a more reliable feed-back position sensor for their hydraulic control systems to replace the existing potentiometers. The potentiometer was a resistive device with a moving contact subject to wear and consequently had a short life particularly with hydraulic system dither. This dither became severe with the advent of high-performance jet aircraft which required more responsive control systems. Since the LVDT was a non-contacting device and it would operate on the 400 Hz power supplies used in high performance aircraft I thought it would be a perfect replacement. The bad news was that the currently available LVDTs were very long devices for the linear stroke available, due primarily to the way coil windings were designed and were not a form-fit-function replacement for the resistive devices. As I thought about the opportunity, I determined that a non-linear winding design could possibly achieve the stroke to length ratio desired by the current military designers.

To test my hypothesis, I contacted an acquantance who was an MIT graduate and had started his own business manufacturing electronic timers using the new transistor technology. His name was Gary Collins and he agreed to build a prototype coil winding according to my instructions. Within a week he called to tell me he had a prototype for me to assess. The results were fantastic, my entrepreneuial genes kicked in, and I convinced him to finish the packaging of the prototype device. Since Chance Vought Aircraft Company in Texas had issued an open invitation to bid on potentiometer replacements for one of their military aircraft, I contacted them with a solution to their problem and they asked for a prototype immediately. Their test results indicated our device met all of their performance requirements.

This led to an initial purchase order for several hundred LVDT position sensors contingent upon our facility evaluation by their contracts team. In the interim, I had convinced Gary and some of my co-workers at Douglas Aircraft to invest as shareholders in a proposed incorporation of Gary's company. Since Gary had no capital of his own, I arranged for him to count his working time at an agreed hourly rate as equivalent investment dollars. Now that Chance Vought wanted to visit our new company to evaluate our ability to perform under their contact, what to do! Gary was the only employee and we had no other business or products under manufacture which did not bode well for a successful audit. On the date of their visit, I convinced my investor colleagues to take the day off from their regular jobs to portray engineering and production staff replete with work benches and test equipment. The audit was successful and we were off and running with this being only the first of many future contracts for our new LVDT product. Unfortunately, we were unable to patent this new device because we naively began selling the product prior to the patent application which negated our position of sole ownership of the technology. This technology now generates annual private business sales to the aerospace market that exceeds $100M with G.L. Collins and Kavlico being the major manufacturers.

The company was growing fast with the demand for these particular aerospace sensors by several other aircraft manufacturers. Gary needed assistance badly so I resigned my job at Douglas Aircraft and became the Vice President of Marketing at our new company, G.L. Collins Corporation. After about five years, we had moved into a new building with some twenty employees, which alas were mostly Gary's friends and relatives. Gary refused to expand the business to accommodate increasing demand since it would dilute his personal control of every aspect of the business. This led to some contention between us and since he had majority control, by virtue of the endless hours he used to pay for his shares, I resigned to pursue other interests.

One of the LVDT companies whose products I used at Douglas Aircraft was called Schaevitz Engineering located in Pennsauken, New Jersey and was founded by Herman Schaevitz some dozen years earlier. They had the lions share of the industrial sensor business but excluding military products and were incapable of competing with G.L. Collins sensors in this specialized market area. When Herman learned about my resignation, he contacted me with an invitation to visit his company in New Jersey and discuss a possible relationship. This I did and it resulted in the formation of Schaevitz West located in Anaheim, California under my management control. We proceeded to sell Schaevitz products in California as well as design special LVDTs with integral electronics and to pursue certain military contracts that exceeded their current capability in New Jersey.

Unfortunately, the Schaevitz parent company had made too many bad acquisitions and they were soon having serious cash flow problems. These included a California machine shop, two start-up companies in Massachusets as well as a Philadelphia company making obsolete measuring instruments. Herman Schaevitz called me in 1963 to ask if I would move to Pennsauken as their General Manager to help him sort out a solution to their financial problems. So, after two years in Anaheim, I agreed to pack up and move to the Pennsauken headquarters along with a few of my key employees and became VP & General Manager of the Schaevitz parent company. But first I was asked to sell one of their California acquisitions, a machine shop in Burbank. What I knew about machine shops you could stick in your ear, nonetheless I soon found a willing buyer and a deal was made.

Although I was determined to stay in California forever, this was an opportunity I could not resist and off we went to New Jersey - myself, my wife, a son, a German Shepard dog & important possessons shoe-horned into our 4-door Cadillac. On the way, my thirteen year old son slipped on a wet sidewalk and broke an arm while walking our dog. This required emergency medical service resulting in a cast on his arm which he reluctantly displayed as an eighth grade student in his new school. Our remaining possessions followed by moving van and ended up in storage until we had a suitable residence. Our first month at my new business location was spent in a local motel until we could find permanent housing. We ultimately ended up in Moorestown, New Jersey, which was an affluent Quaker community and we were well pleased.

My new job required an inventory of key personnel with their strengths and weaknesses so I could assess the people skills. Luckily, they were for the most part extremely competent and I soon established a good working relationship with all of them. Unfortunately, each product manager operated as an independent product-line business but operating out of the same facility, each with their own systems and procedures. This was counter-productive and wasteful so I began working on a centralized organization so it could respond as one company with a classical organization chart. A few of the operations were losers and required some major surgery to separate the wheat from the chaff. Within a year we were back on course with product offerings that reflected our basic technologies only and not ancillary diversions. As a result the negative cash flow problems subsided.

All of the remote acquisitions were sold which further reduced our cash flow problems but not before the bank insisted on a management restructuring to give them confidence in continuing a line of credit. The end result was my appointment as President of Schaevitz Engineering with many years of heady responsibilities ahead. The basic business sales volume after selling unprofitable operations was about $1.5M in 1966 (Pennsauken sensor products primarily).

The business grew modestly over the next several years although our technical prowess improved considerably and by 1975 we were at a sales level of about $5M. In the interim, we acquired full control of a U.K. company, with whom we had a joint venture and minor ownership position, and whose sales level was about $1M. During this period, Herman Schaevitz maintained legal control with a majority of the shares and the position of CEO – although he deferred to me on most operational issues he insisted that product development have priority over sales & marketing.

Consequently, we designed many products that did not meet market demands which wasted cash and permitted only a minimal growth rate. Herman could not resist his personal involvement in all company operations which created some grim encounters over my authority and responsibilities. This seems to be a general problem with entrepreneurs who establish wonderful start-up companies but cannot reach the next step of organization & delegation that will create a world class company – I had the same problem at G.L. Collins. This was a period, when in utter frustration, I limited my working hours to the bare necessities and took time to obtain a private pilots license along with my high school son, Drew.

A particularly significant event occurred in 1968 during a review of a publication frequently perused by our technical staff named, "Hydraulics & Pneumatics" which covered applications for actuators and equipment using hydraulic or pneumatic media – a prime market for our sensor products.. An article appeared in the September issue entitled, "Transducer Elements: Heart of the Newest Measuring Instruments" authored by Edward E. Herceg. This was followed by another of his articles in the December issue entitled, "Five Ways to Use Transducers". These were exceptionally well written technical articles by someone obviously well versed in sensor technologies. I discussed these articles with Herman Schaevitz and suggested we pursue similar articles to promote our own particular technologies. He concurred and we jointly decided to contact Mr. Herceg to ascertain if he would be agreeable to write articles for our company.

Not only did Ed Herceg concur but suggested writing a book about sensor technologies in general with specific chapters show-casing our own products and technologies. In 1972, we published the "Schaevitz Handbook of Measurement and Control" which was disseminated to our customers and field sales personnel. It became a best seller, so to speak, with some 100,000 copies in circulation throughout the world and with many used in college curricula.

As we worked with Ed on this publication, it became clear that here was someone with an extraordinary grasp of electro-mechanical engineering but, in addition, had an excellent grasp of application engineering over a wide range of industries. We soon decided this was someone who should be a member of our technical group and in 1973 he was hired as our Chief Engineer. Eventually he became our Chief Application Engineer and was instrumental in expanding our business into new markets and technologies. He later became an employee in our new company, Macro Sensors.

Eventually, I decided that with the constant second guessing by Herman Schaevitz, this was not a good long term career for me, therefore I resigned and moved back to California to pursue other opportunities. This caused considerable angst among the company directors as well as our U.K. manager and they tried very hard to persuade me to stay but I was adamant and persisted with my move.

I relocated to Newport Beach, California and formed a consulting company, Corporate Development, ensconced in an up-scale corporate office center. Along with some former acquaintances we provided management and technical support to several new companies in the Southern California area as well as some well established concerns. One of my neighbors in our office building was James Roosevelt, son of past-president Franklin D. Roosevelt, and I did some consulting work with him which resulted in an invitation to a yacht club function to hobnob with various yacht-owning movie stars. During this period of time, Herman Schaevitz would call me on a regular basis to complain about his managers and their poor decisions – at one point he contracted with me to come back for a week to help him sort out various problems. Finally, about a year later, he informed me that his wife had filed for a divorce and as part of their settlement he would resign his position but with certain conditions. Both warring parties asked me to return as President with full authority over all operations and with a substantial salary improvement – but with the caveat that I mediate the on-going family negotiations. I was confident I could do that so I accepted forthwith and moved back to Moorestown, NJ.

So here I was, full circle, but with full authority to manage the company as I thought appropriate. Although the mediation role became much more complicated than expected with Herman consistently upping the ante for his departure, within a few weeks we had a settlement. Herman's son, Howard, was appointed as CEO and together we converted the company from a solely technology driven company to a market driven company with superior technologies. Howard was able to almost single handedly set up a competent sales force throughout the United States using independent sales representatives. He did the same in Europe and we were honored by the U.S. Department of Commerce with an E-Award for our excellence in export sales. Howard assumed responsibility for our foreign business operations and I concentrated on our strategic planning as well as implementation domestically. Nonetheless, I became involved when strategic direction was required abroad and particularly when we acquired a French company that was a strong competitor there. This required travel to Europe several times a year to try to integrate corporate modus-operandi which was like trying to pour molasses in January. Dealing with the French (government as well as employees) became intolerable and after a few years the French operations were sold. We retained our UK company however with mixed success in integrating policies and strategies.

Early in its evolution, the company executed a labor agreement with the local Teamsters Union which generally involved successive three year contracts and one of my tasks was conducting contract negotiations with various union negotiators. I had some experience in these negotiations when Herman Schaevitz would include me in prior negotiations. My hot button with the union negotiators was their insistence that workers be paid the same rate of pay regardless of skill levels and that only seniority should determine higher pay scales – I eventually convinced them that skill level as well as seniority should both be used to establish compensation. Several times I was involved in federal mediation to resolve sticky issues in pending contracts. We were now involved in substantial military related contracts and it required us to meet stringent EEOC guidelines and also included periodic drug testing if we wanted to remain as a qualified contractor. At one time, we had feedback from some workers that there was a drug ring operating under our noses so I hired an undercover investigator to work in our machine shop to ferret out any suspects. He found that our black union steward was the dealer and that presented two problems – the union and the EEOC. In addition, the undercover investigator refused to get involved in a battle to prosecute the suspect since it was too time consuming and the respective government attorneys were always at odds with each other with uncertain outcomes. What to do! I had earlier created a new department to service customer product complaints and returns which required some technical skills, in addition I put the union steward in charge of this department – so I decided to eliminate the department and lay off the union steward which satisfied union contract provisions and kept the government at bay.

We were very successful in developing new products and complementary technologies which moved the company into a position of world leadership in a variety of sensors with aggregate sales of about $25M in 1985 and we became an attractive target for acquisition by several large companies – both US and UK concerns that had become very aware of the potential markets for sensor products. We declined to pursue negotiations with any of the interested companies. In 1985 we had just completed the preliminary development of a unique position sensor that could be manufactured in large quantities at a very low cost and formed a new subsidiary company, Sensor Technologies, Inc, to complete the development of marketable products for high volume applications such as trucks & off-road vehicles. One of the companies interested in buying these products for motor vehicle applications was Lucas Industries, Plc. located in the UK and we spent considerable time discussing mutually acceptable terms & conditions for a long term relationship. On one of their visits to our corporate headquarters Howard Schaevitz and I were at lunch with their negotiating team when they indicated they would like to buy our company and made an offer of $20M. This was very close to the estimate of company value I had given to our board of directors at a recent meeting.

This began a series of events that could best be termed mind-boggling since we now had to contact all of the companies who had approached us earlier but we had declined to pursue their interests – this was a necessary step since we were a public company and were obligated to optimize shareholder value As a result, a bidding war began which lasted several months and ended with Lucas as the highest bidder at $33M which was about equal to our total annual sales at that time. Consequently, in late 1986 the company was sold to Lucas Industries, Plc and we became employees of a UK company leaving some very rich Schaevitz family members and substantial rewards for some key managers who participated in a company stock ownership plan (ESOT). However, Lucas corporate policy was to force retirement of all executive level managers when they reached the age of 62 years so that new blood could be infused into the management pool. Since I was already 62 years old at the time, they made an exception in my case so that I could assist with the transition of management control – my retirement age was extended to age 65 (July 22, 1990).

Lucas immediately took control of our new development company, Sensor Technologies, Inc. and moved all operations to England to expedite the manufacture of these low cost sensors for the motor vehicle market. Unfortunately, they overlooked some key technical personnel associated with this new product and after investing over $1M in new facilities they were unsuccessful in commercializing this technology. They eventually abandoned this program and some of the employees left to pursue the products independently. Luckily, they still had the products we had commercialized in the US using these patented technologies which were producing annual sales levels of about $1M. The Lucas management competency left a lot to be desired and when I retired in 1990 company growth had essentially ceased and was now on a downward trend.

My retirement included a 3-year non-compete agreement so I resurrected my former consulting business but with a new company name, International Business Network (IBN), with the goal of helping European companies gain access to US markets and conversely for US companies to gain access to European markets. Most of my consulting activities involved US companies who were intrigued with the remarkable growth of Schaevitz Engineering and were interested in my secrets to success.

Unfortunately, comparable success meant not only strategic planning but appropriate investment to succeed and most of my clients were unwilling to take this step – some were willing but only if I joined them as the project manager which I was unwilling to do considering the long distance moves involved, not to mention my age at the time and non-compete restrictions.

In 1994, I learned that Lucas U.S. management had decided to consolidate most of their US operations in Hampton, Virginia to take advantage of certain tax exemptions and subsidies for companies offering local job opportunities. Accordingly, all of the Schaevitz U.S. operations along with other U.S. companies were consolidated in new Hampton facilities with little synergy between the various entities. The decision was made to move only a few of the key people from our former company and some 150 employees were left in the parking lot without jobs. Worst of all, they left some of the most critical and experienced design and management personnel who were absolutely key to their future success. I was astounded by this decision but could do nothing about it.

Shortly, I was contacted by three of these key former employees to see if I would help them form a new company to compete with our former company, Schaevitz Engineering. I agreed to meet with them and ascertain the prospects for such a venture and I discovered that none had signed non-compete agreements. My non-compete agreement had also expired by then. They were willing to sacrifice current incomes for future gains and the three entrepreneurs included the very best designer of inductive sensor products, the best manager of manufacturing and one of the very good marketing managers. This combination of skills and expectations was a good predictor of success so I put together a strategic business plan that outlined the products, marketing techniques and cash requirements needed to start up and grow a new business venture. Although this entrepreneurial group were expert in their particular area of experience none had any experience in either forming a company or providing the management skills to be both legal and successful. They asked if I would assume the position of president during start up and I agreed assuming we could come up with the funds for this purpose. My business plan estimated we needed approximately $500K to achieve a self generating revenue status even with zero or marginal compensation for the new owners. Unfortunately, only two of us had any reserve cash positions to apply to the venture so I looked for another partner with deep pockets – Howard Schaevitz with his extensive proceeds from the Lucas sale came to the rescue.

To be absolutely fair to the original group, I came up with a shareholders agreement that offered a 51% ownership position to Howard Schaevitz and the balance of 49% split equally among the four remaining shareholders (myself included) with the caveat that each of us would put up cash for each share proportional to the percentage of ownership. Howard and I paid for our shares up front and the other three were to pay as soon as their payroll income provided the funds, however until the company was self sufficient none would receive a pay check but an equal and competitive wage would be recorded as future deferred compensation. We reached unanimous agreement and the Howard A. Schaevitz Technologies company was incorporated in the State of New Jersey in December, 1994 to be operated under the name of Macro Sensors (dba).

I immediately rented office space in a building about three blocks from home, bought some used furniture, acquired a business computer with financial accounting software and the five of us shared space in our 600 square foot facility beginning in early

January, 1995. Our initial share purchase capitalization was about $250,000 which was less than my business plan requirement, however Howard agreed to loan the company additional working capital at a competitive interest rate. Initial products were designed, manufactured and promoted within six months from start up resulting in a growing order backlog from previous customers who understood we were the original team that provided some of their prior products. Our first employee was a woman who worked with us at our former company and she became our interim office manager

I had leased the original office space for a 12-month period and by the time our lease was due to expire we had outgrown the facility and we subsequently moved into a 5,000 square foot facility in Pennsauken, NJ with a 3-year lease. This began a very rapid growth of the business and the addition of several other former employees but more importantly paychecks for the owners. Howard and I opted to defer our compensation for an additional two years to conserve cash for operations. We also purchased more equipment and invested in many leasehold improvements which necessitated borrowing about $100K from Howard Schaevitz on a long term note. By the time this lease was due to expire we had outgrown this facility as well and we searched for another facility with a minimum of 10,000 square feet of operating space. A 16,000 square foot facility was leased in an industrial park near our current facility and I was able to negotiate a sub-lease with the current tenant for about 4,000 square feet of space so we ended up with an optimum sized new space at a very competitive leasing cost.

In our eleventh year of business (2006) our sales level had reached more than $2,750,000 per annum and after negotiating with three competing companies, we sold the business to another New Jersey sensor company known as American Sensor Technologies, Inc. (AST) who were at about the same sales level. Interestingly, all of the bidding companies were operated by personnel who were former Schaevitz Engineering employees or colleagues we were conversant with over the years. We sold the company for about $4M which exceeded our projected sales level in the following year and, fortunately, the facility with all employees remained intact which bodes well for the future of the combined companies.

So now, in retrospect, my 55-years in the business world was a fantastic journey and I often wondered how it happened to me. I think being born in the twentieth century and being at the right place at the right time with marketable skills were important factors.

My desire and ability to deal with competent and innovative technical persons, prima-donnas to some extent, was important on the path I followed in my business career. Also recognizing that matching personnel to job descriptions was an imperfect exercise – always there were areas of individual strengths and areas of individual weaknesses and managers must optimize the strengths and supplement the weaknesses.

There seems to be an innate competition between departments in every company relative to whose contribution is the most important to business success – whether it be engineering, manufacturing or marketing. A successful manager must keep everything in perspective and be a facilitator of team efforts. Above all, in a manufacturing business, the executive level manager must understand the design & manufacturing technologies involved, the vital role of sales & marketing and must have a vision of future trends in customer demand. This was my challenge and opportunity which made my career so rewarding.

H. Schaevitz

L. Bondy

LETTER TO STOCKHOLDERS

LETTER TO STOCKHOLDERS

We welcome this opportunity to explain to our shareholder friends why we expect a logical continuation of our present growth.

As predicted last year, 1972 exhibited a substantial rise in sales and profit ending with an increase in volume of some 30% over 1971 figures. Net income is 23¢ per share compared to 0.6¢ per share in 1971.

We feel our increased penetration of the industrial measurement and control market, particularly in the automation areas, is primarily responsible for our recent progress.

It is our intention to pursue these markets even more diligently, both foreign and domestic, through increased marketing and development activities. Towards this end, the following steps have already been taken:

(1) Publication of a "Schaevitz Handbook of Measurement and Control" to help promote our products worldwide.

(2) Completion of a European sales plan to increase our market penetration in that area.

(3) Appointment of a Western Regional Sales Manager to increase our market penetration in the Western U.S.A.

(4) An aggressive development program to improve our proprietary product position in the areas of electronic weighing and automatic gaging.

Subsequent to our last Annual Meeting, four officers were appointed to new positions by the Board of Directors: LeRoy A. Bondy, President; Howard A. Schaevitz, Vice President of Marketing; Joseph Lipshutz, Vice President of Operations; and, Ruth J. Norwitz, Assistant Secretary/Treasurer. All were appointed from within the ranks of the company and no major change in management philosophy is contemplated. Herman Schaevitz remains active as Chairman of the Board and Chief Executive Officer.

Performance during the early months of 1973 indicates increased growth during the ensuing year.

Since our product and market base has expanded considerably during the past few years, we are including in this report a brief summary of your company's activities in the World's marketplace.

Herman Schaevitz
Chairman of the Board

LeRoy A. Bondy
President

LETTER TO
SHAREHOLDERS

Howard A. Schaevitz
Chairman of the Board

LeRoy A. Bondy
President

For Schaevitz Engineering, calendar year 1985 marked a period of intense strategic planning and resource consolidation as we look ahead to the market opportunities of the next ten years. During this past year, we continued the implementation of our previously reported plan for separating our U.S. operation into two distinct groups – engineered products for aerospace markets and standard catalog products for the industrial market. While examining our overseas operations, however, we found that the combined effects of a divergent local management philosophy and an unfavorable business climate in France made for a poor fit with our overall plans. Consequently, we decided to divest the French operations in late 1985.

The company's consolidated 1985 sales increased 5% to $23,639,000, compared to $22,552,000 in 1984. For purposes of comparison, the effect of French operations has been eliminated from both years. Sales for U.S. operations alone increased 6¾% to $18,561,000, compared with $17,385,000 in 1984.

In the past year, a substantial portion of management's effort was directed toward labor relation activities, with some sacrifice in the short-term performance of the company. The culmination of this effort was that in the fall of 1985, the members of the bargaining unit at Schaevitz Engineering voted to decertify their labor union in an NLRB-supervised election. We believe this extraordinary action has paved the way for an era of vastly improved labor relations with our workforce and long-term stability for the company.

As part of the company's efforts to foster these improved labor relations, we have decided to change our accounting system from a calendar-year basis to a fiscal-year basis, beginning April 1st, 1986. The fiscal year will be April 1 through March 31. We believe this action will alleviate the conflict that previously existed between the company's year-end production demands and our workers' family and social commitments during the holiday season. For the stub year, January 1st, 1986 through March 31st, 1986, U.S. sales were $4,560,000, compared to $3,107,000 for the same period in the previous year.

As part of our long-term growth strategy, early in 1985 we established a subsidiary research and development company, Sensor Technologies, Inc. (STI). This affiliate is aggressively pursuing the development of several new proprietary products for both our traditional markets and for the worldwide markets for sensors at large that we have not been able to penetrate before.

For fiscal 1986-1987, our outlook is very positive. We feel that the consolidation activities of the past year have focused our market perspectives as well as strengthened our financial position. Our sophisticated technology base has permitted us to expand further in the worldwide aerospace market. Our well-established name in the industrial marketplace continues to help us gain an increased share of the general economic growth in the U.S. and our investment in alternate sensor technologies has poised us to exploit the burgeoning mass markets for sensors. Bolstered by these positive actions, we are moving forward with confidence and optimism.

Howard A. Schaevitz
Chairman of the Board

LeRoy A. Bondy
President

Macro Sensors
Executive Resume

Name:	Lee Bondy
Current Title:	President
Date:	January 1, 2004

A. Background Summary
Over 50 years of progressively responsible positions in high-technology businesses including engineering, engineering management, sales & marketing management, manufacturing management and general management.

B. Areas of Expertise

1. P&L Responsibility
2. Strategic Planning
3. Market Planning
4. Technology Planning
5. International Ventures
6. Multi-division Management
7. Financial Planning
8. Cost Analysis & Control

C. Key Accomplishments

1. Successful initiation and management of several new companies.
2. Acquisition and operation of foreign companies.
3. Negotiated & administered several license agreements.
4. Implementation of several new-product development programs.
5. Initiated and monitored strategic & tactical business plans.
6. President and COO of leading sensor companies for 35+ years.

D. Professional History

1995-Present	Co-founder and President of Macro Sensors
1990-1995	Independent Consultant (IBN)
1989-1990	Executive consultant to Lucas, plc.
1963-1989	President & COO of Schaevitz Engineering

1958-1963	Co-founder and Vice President of G.L. Collins Corp.
1952-1958	Engineering group manager with Douglas Aircraft Co.

E. Military Service and Education

1943-1946	U.S. Navy Radar Technician (WW2)
1946-1950	Graduated with BEE degree from U of Minnesota
1950-1952	Electronics Instructor USN (Korean Conflict)
1960-1962	MBA, University of California

F. Avocations

1. Private pilot SEL with instrument rating and member of local flying club.
2. Lions Club member and officer.

Macro Sensors Founders

Front row-Howard Schaevitz (left) & Lee Bondy (right)

Back row-left to right – Rich Anderson,
Gene Anderson & Jim Lang

Macro Sensors founders at a Company picnic

Left to right – Howard Schaevitz, Harold Schaevitz,

Rich Anderson, Lee Bondy & Ed Herceg

At a Chicago manufacturing trade show

Replica of the Schaevitz

"Handbook of Measurement and Control"

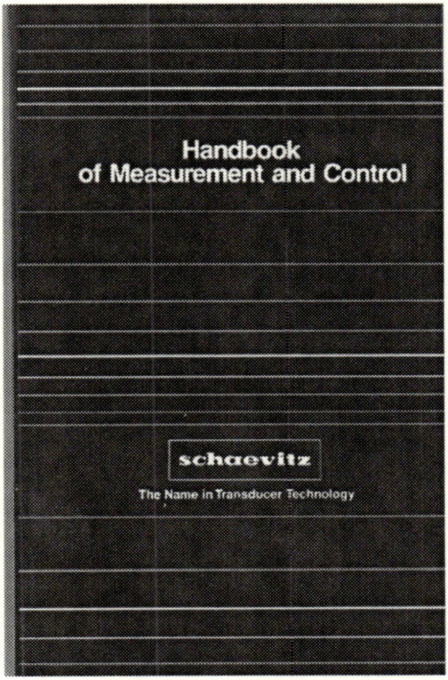

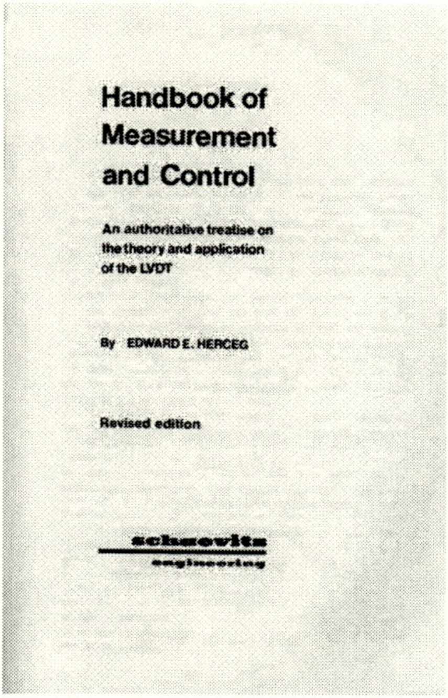

Inside cover of Handbook

Chapter 8 – Love & Marriage

"Love & marriage go together like a horse & carriage.."

Growing up pretty much isolated from the opposite sex during my rural isolation, girls were not on my radar screen until late in my high school years. Unlike the early age dating phenomenon of today.

There were several young women in our Bemidji high school social group but no steady dating took place. Although there was one girl in particular with whom I felt a close bond and vice versa. She faithfully corresponded with me during my WWII Navy service commitment and we dated steadily after I returned home. She had just finished high school when I departed for the University of Minnesota in the Twin Cities and our contacts gradually diminished to zero.

My parting advice from close relatives when I left Bemidji for the U of M was to be careful in the big city and be aware of Catholic girls because marrying one would put me under control of the Pope who would insist I have as many children as my Uncle K.K. in Montana.

Since I had now discovered the female part of society, in my sophomore year in college I was dating a nursing student regularly. She lived in an all female dormitory (no co-educational living quarters in those days) and getting beyond the lobby was like getting into Fort Knox. Nonetheless, we enjoyed college activities together and it seemed we were destined for a long-term relationship. Fortunately or unfortunately, she graduated a year before I was to graduate and accepted a job in California. Our contacts diminished to zero. It was then that I met another nursing student from a Catholic school dormitory during a mixer with students from other schools and I was mesmerized after an evening with her – she gave me her private phone number and I planned to arrange another date but after thinking about the warning from my family I left well enough alone and never called.

At the end of my Junior year I resumed my usual Summer job of cleaning & painting vacated dormitory residences in preparation for the next school term. There were several Summer students from colleges outside of the State of Minnesota who attended some specialized education classes at the U of M. The university planned several social events for these Summer students and since we were students as well, although on Summer work assignment, we were permitted to attend these functions. One of the events was a river paddle-boat cruise on the Mississippi River with dinner & dancing – my roommate had reservations and a date with one of the Summer students but had no money so I took his place and shortly met my blind date. She was Wilma Williams and a teacher from Cambridge, Ohio attending U of M special education classes. We bonded immediately, enjoyed our cruise as well as many other dates until she left at Summers end to resume her teaching career in Ohio.

This was a relationship that did not fade like Summer roses and we were in regular contact thereafter. I was invited to visit with her and her family during my Senior year Christmas break and on one of our dates I proposed marriage which she accepted immediately. After receiving her parents blessing, the wedding was subsequently planned to occur soon after my graduation.

My new bride-to-be along with a younger Sister, Martha Anne, lived in the home of their Aunt, Lillian Green, who's husband,

Harry Green, was the county engineer. It seems her Father died some years earlier and her Mother didn't want responsibility for the children so a court order gave the Green's custody of both girls. Although, technically, the Greens' were not their legally adoptive parents, for all intents and purposes they fulfilled all parental obligations and provided extraordinary love and affection to the two sisters. Each received musical training and both graduated from an Ohio teachers college. In retrospect, you could say they were somewhat spoiled.

I graduated from the U of M on June 10, 1950, with a job waiting for me in Cleveland, Ohio, we were married on June 25, 1950 and honeymooned in Niagra Falls, NY. Coincidently, the Korean Conflict began on the date of our marriage which would soon impact our life immensely.

We moved into an apartment in a suburb of Cleveland (Parma) and I began working as a design engineer with the ECM Company which manufactured electric motor controls. My wife was hired by the Parma school district as an elementary teacher. This new job was my first taste of regular employment in my chosen profession and I liked it very much. The ECM Company was shortly acquired by the Reliance Electric Corporation and I transferred to their electric motor design group.

As noted in Chapter 6, in October, 1950 I was recalled into the regular Navy to serve during the Korean Conflict. This turned our life style upside down and soon I was back in uniform. After induction I was sent to the Naval Training Center in San Diego for instructor training with my wife and our Studebaker wagon along for the ride.

After my graduation from the instructor training center I was assigned to teach radar & sonar technology to seamen in Ohau, Hawaii. There was some uncertainty with Naval brass whether my wife could join me in Hawaii but finally it was approved and they agreed to ship my automobile as well. Soon my wife was on an airline heading for Hawaii followed by my automobile on a Navy transport ship and I was on another Navy transport ship (a slow boat to China adventure). I arrived after my wife but before my automobile but finally assembled and found an apartment on Waikiki Beach to resume a somewhat normal life albeit with Navy duty demands and restrictions. My wife subsequently became an elementary school teacher of navy personnel dependent children.

During my 18-month duty period in Hawaii my wife became pregnant with our first child. Unfortunately, there was confusion on the part of the Navy medical staff over whether this was really a pregnancy or some other malady. The Navy medical care in that era was focused primarily on male and not female ailments with no gynecologists on the staff. The doctors first prescribed hormone therapy to induce a menstrual period with no success and finally took x-rays which revealed a developing fetus. As she approached full term the Navy brass decided to send her to the Navy Hospital in San Diego and I was given leave to accompany her. We obtained seats on a Navy PBY amphibious airplane and after a 10-hour flight we touched down in San Diego harbor. My wife delivered a baby boy in the Naval hospital in November, however he was born with a serious heart defect and we never took him home. He would require constant medical care in a local nursing home in San Diego..

I received an early discharge from my Navy service and we scrambled to find local employment to be near our sickly child and to pay for his outpatient care. In today's litigious world the Navy would be held responsible for medical malpractice for incompetent medical services.

As noted in Chapter 7, we moved to Long Beach, California where I worked as an engineer at the Douglas Aircraft Corporation and my wife found a job teaching in a local elementary school. Our first residence was an efficiency apartment with minimum facilities. Our bedroom was a fold-down wall bed in the living room along with a small kitchen and one bathroom. Not elegant but affordable which enhanced our cash flow. Within 6-months our first- born died and was buried in a San Diego cemetery.

The adage that you are also married to your spouse's relatives came true and soon my wife's sister, Martha Ann, and her husband, Jim, moved to Long Beach, California. They had a young child, Jimmie, who stayed with us often on weekends when his parents were sightseeing in the West. Sometimes, they vanished and we did not know where they could be reached and they rarely ever returned on the specified time or day. This left us with family responsibilities early on.

On September 30, 1953, our second Son, Drew, was born and it changed our lifestyle forever. He was my pride and joy who I enjoyed from childhood to adulthood. We bought a two bedroom home in one of the new developments in Lakewood, California which was adjacent to Long Beach. We now had the typical problem of juggling two jobs with our parenting duties which was exacerbated by babysitting our little nephew Jimmie on occasion.

We lived in Southern California at a time of extraordinary population growth and soon hundreds of acres of orange groves were bull-dozed to make way for large new home developments that grew like mushrooms. When Disney acquired a large tract of land to build Disney World, it was soon surrounded by new homes and businesses. Every month models for new homes were opened for inspection and before long we purchased a larger more elegant home in Anaheim using the equity in our Lakewood home to make the down payment. This was an ongoing trend in Southern California with home owners constantly selling and upgrading.

Within a year my wife's parents retired and also moved to Anaheim, purchasing a duplex property that provided supplemental income. They wanted to be near their new grandchildren although an older grandson still lived in Cambridge, Ohio. They were wonderful Christian people who doted on their children and grandchildren. They became our permanent baby sitters. Her father died in 1958 and her mother was left with a duplex to manage on her own. To assist her, I spent a lot of time helping with the maintenance of the property.

Unfortunately, my wife's mother developed incurable cancer and she soon required constant home nursing care. She chose me to be her legal guardian with the authority to manage her financial affairs. This required the employment of around the clock nursing care which I found and employed. In the beginning the siblings would take turns monitoring their mothers condition. All went well for a while but soon the siblings were quarreling over one thing or another. Before long, another daughter who still lived in Cambridge, Ohio came to California and joined the fracas. I did my best to mediate the disputes but they continued to escalate and I was caught in the middle trying to accomplish my guardian duties.

Their actions were astounding to me and on occasion I had to reprimand them for acting this way in the proximity of their dying mother. At one point, I went to Martha Ann's home, rang the doorbell and when she answered I said I was here to mediate a dispute – the response was a punch in the face which broke my eyeglasses and cut my face. I returned home holding one good eyepiece in one hand to see the road and driving with the other hand. So here I was, attacked by all the siblings, including my wife, for trying to be neutral and fair while looking after their mother's best interests.

I was on a business trip to the Northeast in 1965 when my wife called to say her mother had died and the sisters were arguing over which mortuary they would use. Could I come home immediately and exercise my authority to settle the matter. Returning home the next day I discovered my wife's other two sisters had made a preemptive move and moved their mother's body to the mortuary of their choice. Needless to say, the civil war raged on and the wheels of the marriage carriage were about to come off.

Finally their mother was buried and her possessions distributed in accordance with her will which was intended to placate them all. Unfortunately, the property was left in equal proportion to the three sisters. I suggested that the property should be sold with the proceeds placed in separate trust funds for the future education of the three grandsons. The two older sisters agreed but the youngest, Martha Ann, refused and insisted on managing the property herself to reap a larger reward in the future – so we acquiesced. She soon discovered that the neighborhood was changing and the only tenants available were Mexican immigrants who soon destroyed the property by filling each of the apartments with multiple families.

In the meantime, I was packing to leave for my new position in Pennsauken, New Jersey. I soon settled into my job with great enthusiasm with much responsibility but boundless opportunities. My wife was away from her siblings and decided to forego her teaching career to concentrate on her music avocation. She had a well trained Coloratura Soprano voice and soon found a local music teacher to develop her voice for a professional career. I always supported her goals and attended all of her private and public concerts. On one occasion arranging to transport a grand piano to Glassboro, New Jersey for a program with her own pianist. All concerts were gratis and the prospects of earning money for performances were nil. Nonetheless the marriage was now calm and Drew was completing his last two years of High School

In Drew's junior year of high school he came home one day and said, "Dad, I joined the high school flying club and I am going to take flying lessons. One of the math-teachers is also a flight instructor." Well, I was apprehensive at first and then decided to attend some evening ground school courses for budding pilots to investigate this crazy idea. Before long I was hooked as well and the rest is history as we both achieved our private pilot licenses in September, 1970 when Drew was 16 years of age and I was 45 years of age.

Soon Drew was in college at Arizona State pursuing an aviation career and joined the Air Force ROTC. He came home during Summer recess and we had the opportunity to fly together. Upon graduation, he was accepted for pilot training at the Williams AFB in Arizona. After completion of his pilot training, he flew KC135 air refueling tankers in the Air Force Reserve then later flew C-130 aircraft in the Air National Guard until his service commitment ended.

Shortly thereafter, I resigned my position at Schaevitz Engineering and returned to California for about a year – see Chapter 7. We bought property in Newport Beach, California and settled in for a new life in our favorite State. My wife insisted we live in a nice home, which in that area, was very expensive and while trying to establish a new business, cash requirements were very high. Fortunately we still owned an acre of land in an exclusive area near Anaheim called Peralta Hills and we sold it at an extremely good price. Our social life was pretty dull except for some events at the Newport Beach yacht club and occasional visits from our friends in the East.

Finally, I received the call from Herman Schaevitz with an offer to return to my former position with a welcome promise of laissez-faire and we headed back to New Jersey. Our house in Moorestown was still on the market so we moved back in – almost like awakening from a long sleep. Our business grew rapidly with Herman replaced by Howard as CEO and we soon exceeded $20 million dollars in sales level (see Chapter 7).

This required much more time at work and regular trips to Europe which made my wife very unhappy. She felt that when you reached the executive levels your time was spent playing golf and going on long vacations, which is just the opposite of reality. I tried very hard to support her musical aspirations but really knew nothing about the music business except that few made any money. Nonetheless, we usually had weekends and annual vacations together with a good income to support a good lifestyle. She at one time decided to attend the Academy of Music in Vienna and insisted I take a leave of absence from my job and accompany her during the school term. Of course, I had a very responsible position and further, it would be impractical to forego the income required for such an event. Needless to say, she stormed off without me and returned a few months later.

Her constant unrealistic demands and a relationship with a third person (male) soon led to irreconcilable differences and the wheels came off the "marriage carriage." in early-1982. We were then involved with divorce proceedings that involved several of my wife's attorneys (consecutive) that finally concluded on June 2, 1983 in the Burlington County courthouse.

During these long divorce proceedings, I met a wonderful woman at a singles dance which grew into an engagement and then a marriage on June 10, 1983. Her name is Madeline Schultz and she had a very unhappy previous marriage but together we have lived happily ever after. She has been very supportive of my business responsibilities, has a very accomplished daughter and wonderful extended family. We bought a duplex property in Riverton, New Jersey and her daughter, husband and daughter (our granddaughter) live in one of the duplex apartments – we have a very supportive and loving relationship that makes life worthwhile.

My Son married a lovely and talented local girl, Doreen Derr, on November 1, 1980 and they have two children, Jennifer and Kevin Bondy who were born on November 12, 1985 and November 9, 1987 respectively. My Step-Daughter, Carol Vento, and her husband Frank have one Daughter, Rosemary, born on February 15, 1983. I am very fortunate to have three healthy, talented and responsible grandchildren whom I cherish very much.

Above, Lee Bondy Family – Circa 1961

Below, New Lee Bondy Family – Circa 1994

Left to right – Lee, Madeline, Carol, Rosemary & Frank

Lee & Madeline Bondy – Circa 1994

Drew Bondy at age two

Below right, Drew– Circa 1993

Below left, Doreen Bondy with our grandkids Jennifer & Kevin – Circa 1993

Madeline, Lee & Rosemary –

front Jennifer and Kevin – Circa 1994

Below, Carol's graduation from Rutgers Law School – with Mom & Lee – Circa 1990

Below, Rosemary sunning herself on Grandma's Cadillac

My Sister's 50th wedding anniversary family portrait – Circa 1997

Front row, Sister Phyllis center & Husband Jerry at left

Back row, right to left, Lee Bondy, Roger Bondy & his wife Elisabeth

My Sister and I – Circa 1997

My Niece Becky and I – Circa 1997

Brother Roger and Wife Elisabeth in native costume – Circa 1991

Me, my Brother, Roger and Elisabeth – Circa 1986

Elisabeth & Roger with a plaque honoring 50 yrs of service in their church – Circa 2005

<u>Chapter 9</u> – Avocations

"All work & no play makes Jack a dull boy"

Although I enjoyed sand-lot baseball when growing up in Montana, when I was in my senior year at the University of Minnesota we were offered opportunities to take tennis and golf lessons as a future recreational activity. Along with a few college friends, I began learning the art of golfing and thought this would be a nice hobby after my graduation – all equipment was provided on a loan basis and the golf course was available at a very modest fee. I was married soon after my graduation and my new wife, hearing about my interest in golf, bought me a very nice set of golf clubs. Unfortunately, my life became too hectic and demanding that I never touched the clubs but carried them with me for some future use. Finally, after our third household move I sold them and never looked back.

As I noted in Chapter 7, my son, Drew, got me interested in flying and this began my devoted lifetime avocation. Consequently on September 6, 1970, I passed my private pilot flight test in our Piper trainer which was designated as PA-28-140 with the identification of 1569J which we fondly called 69 Juliet. The very next day, with the family aboard, we flew to Cambridge, Ohio via Zanesville to visit my wife's home town and returned the following day for a round trip flying time of 8 hours. Within two months we flew to my last hometown of Bemidji, Minnesota to visit friends and relatives which covered some 2,500 miles with an overnight stop each way. Drew and I would alternate flying each leg of the trip. We discovered 69 Juliet, which had a cruising speed of about 100 MPH, when confronted with a headwind, barely kept up with road traffic and we subsequently limited our cross country flying to shorter destinations.

In April of 1971 I traded 69J for a Mooney aircraft designated as M20F with the identification of 2975L which became known as 75 Lima. This was one of the fastest single engine airplanes available at that time and had a cruising speed of about 150 MPH which opened up a whole new vista of cross country flying. A trip to Cambridge, Ohio was now about 6 hours round trip and starting in July of 1971 we began to fly to destinations in California, Oregon and Washington State.

Some of our more notable adventures in 75 Lima are highlighted below:

? May 19, 1971 – Drew and I flew to First Flight airport in North Carolina to visit the Wright Brothers museum at Kitty Hawk to do a documentary about the Wright Brothers. Drew had an assignment from one of his high school classes to take the school's 8 mm movie camera and record an important event or personality. The highlight was me flying 75 Lima around the monument to compare the first aircraft with a modern aircraft. He had a classmate who accurately imitated the voice of Walter Conkrite on a tape recorder that was played along with the film – needless to say he received high marks for the project. The film and recording was demonstrated at a New Jersey State aviation seminar and they asked to retain it for other showings – unfortunately it was never returned.

? July 23, 1971 – The family departed for a West Coast adventure via Ohio, Missouri, New Mexico, Arizona, California ending in Tri City, Oregon to visit some relatives. After some local sightseeing flights including a Crater Lake fly-by with excited relatives as passengers, we headed home via Montana and North Dakota with a stop in my hometown of Bemidji, Minnesota for a few days. Then on to our home airport of Red Lion in New jersey via Michigan and Ohio. We arrived home on August 7, 1971 after a grueling trip but very impressed with the travel value and performance of our new aircraft.

? January 29, 1972 – A first Winter flight to Maine to fly around Mt. Washington and return with an over-flight of JFK airport. Picked up some ice over New York but landed safely at Red Lion airport the same day.

? March 23, 1974 – Departed for Phoenix via Kentucky and Texas to stay with Drew who was attending school at Arizona State College with the intention of pursuing my instrument rating on a crash course effort. The weather in New Jersey was very uncertain which precluded flying on a regular basis but in Phoenix I could fly with an instructor on a daily basis which I did. On April 6, 1974 I departed Phoenix and returned to N.E. Philadelphia airport via Texas and Tennessee landing on April 7, 1974. I completed my instrument check ride on May 22, 1974.

? January 14, 1975 – Departed Hammonton, NJ airport for a trip to Washington State via Ohio, Texas, California and Oregon with a stop in Santa Ana, California to visit friends for a few days. Then landing at Kitsap County airport in Washington on January 24, 1975 for a visit with my Brother, Roger, for a few days. Departed Kitsap on January 28, 1975 back to New Jersey via Montana, North Dakota, Wisconsin, Michigan and Pennsylvania arriving at Hammonton on January 29th with a strong northeaster storm with 35 knot winds that prevented a landing at the Hammonton airport. I had to divert to Atlantic City airport and the landing was like riding a bucking bronco to the runway but I was able to get the airplane down safely. Had to stay in a motel overnight and flew home to Hammonton the next day. One of those events a pilot never forgets.

Above, photo of a Mooney similar to the one I owned for some 10-years

Typical of a mountain flight and VFR on-top

Below, me in a new Mooney at the AOPA convention in Atlantic City

Above, visiting with a group of fellow pilots at the AOPA convention

Below, I am admiring the new Cirrus SR-22 all-composite aircraft.

This has become the most popular single engine propeller aircraft in the world.

Chapter 10 –Religion and Politics

"In God we Trust"

My Grandfather, Knute W. Bondy, was a staunch Lutheran parishioner and was involved in the establishment of the Trefoldighed Lutheran Church near Battle Lake, Minnesota. He remained as a director until he died in 1908. He is buried in the church cemetery. My Grandmother made sure all of her children as well as all available grandchildren were properly baptized in their church – I happened to be one of the grandchildren.

Growing up amidst the second generation siblings, I had no sense of the same religious fervor or dedication so my personal understanding of the Lutheran religion or any religion, for that matter, was nil. My Aunt Emma Bondy, matron of the Richland, Montana ranch family, did insist that my twin cousins and I attend a Summer catechism class in Richland. I thereafter got the sense that Christmas and Easter were important holiday events but that is about all that rubbed off on me. There were no celebrated holidays on the ranch since cows had to be milked every day without fail. I never personally witnessed the events, but apparently most of the KK siblings were properly married by a Lutheran pastor.

The Bondy clan politics were conservative to a fault although I don't recall much conversation or debate on the matter. My Grandfather served two terms in the Minnesota legislature as a Republican candidate from the Battle Lake district and his only known photo appeared on his campaign literature (see his photo at the end of Chapter 1). My Father seemed to be very anti-Democratic and consistently criticized the term of Franklin D.

Roosevelt who was President most of my early years. I admired FDR greatly and voted for him once after reaching voting age in WWII and after the war I also voted for Harry Truman who I thought was an excellent President. One of the favorite books in my home library is the "Truman" biography by David M. McCullough. After WWII and completion of my college education I entered into the real world of good citizenship and religion and politics took on a new meaning.

My first wife and her family were long-time Methodists which was alright with me considering I had no other religious proclivity. My wife and some of her relatives were advocates of Spiritualism which I thought was very unscientific. One response to my wife was, "I suppose chickens and cows have spirits too and we eat them."

Settling in California after the Korean Conflict I was exposed to every religion and cult known to man – which seemed to flourish in the California social environment. I was soon intrigued with the religious menu available in California and experimented with a wide gamut of flavors in our spare time. Although my wife was intrigued with the Spiritualist practice of communicating with deceased relatives, I was never comfortable with the translations offered by mediums. Except for the comfort of knowing life and intelligence existed beyond the grave, the communications seemed pointless. No one of any historical importance ever came through with great revelations.

The most intriguing religions to me were the Hindu and Buddhist faiths which seemed to address the confluence of the spiritual and physical person. Proper thoughts and actions were critical to a meaningful life – not too different from most Christian religions albeit with their particular dogma and rituals. I was particularly impressed with Paramahansa Yoganandi's book "The Autobiography of a Yogi" and I visited his retreat several times in California.

As my responsibilities at work and at home grew spare time decreased proportionally, we settled into a more conventional existence and joined the local Methodist Church in Anaheim, California. I became quite active in the church activities and increased our range of friends immensely. At one point I hired a fellow parishioner, Robert Johnson, to work as a sales engineer in our new sensor company, G.L. Collins, Inc. Business and family obligations took precedence over other facets of life so religion as an educational pursuit went on the back burner.

While living in Southern California, I became more aware of local and national politics and attended some of the associated political rallies. The most memorable was a rally at Knots Berry Farm, a popular and local entertainment park on a par with Disneyland, featuring Ronald Reagan who was running for Governor of California. He was a very inspiring speaker and was accompanied by no other than John Wayne, who needed no introduction. This piqued my interest in the battle over ideas and from that time forward I became a staunch conservative – not exactly a die-hard Republican but my vote would go to candidates with moderate, conservative ideas.

Times changed and we moved on to Southern New Jersey settling in the conservative Quaker town of Moorestown. We again joined a neighboring Methodist Church where I continued with various church activities. My wife became increasingly occupied with attending only those churches that allowed her to perform as their soloist. This was also a period when the wheels of the "marriage carriage' were coming loose and religion as well as politics sank into the mud.

After my Son was married and on his own, the first marriage ended and I was soon married to a wonderful, understanding woman who became a very supportive partner in life. I was once again able to pursue the avocations of politics and religion.

During the post-Reagan period, I voted a pure conservative, Republican ticket until Bill Clinton came along. I was intrigued with Clinton's middle of the road stance and his proposed solutions to the Country's various problems, "It's the economy, stupid." He got my vote for the first term, however I was very disillusioned by the time of his second term and I returned to my conservative roots.

My frequent business trips to Europe highlighted the problems with socialistic governments – in particular France with social contracts killing any future for entrepreneurial businesses. Our U.S. company owned a French business for three years but it was impossible to earn a profit in this environment so we sold it to a French national who thought he could out-fox the government. He failed at the business also. I think Calvin Coolidge had the right idea, "The business of government is business."

My trips to Europe made me aware of how lucky we are to live in the USA and without fail when we would touch down at our home airport all US citizens would clap in appreciation and some would kiss the tarmac.

After my first retirement in 1990, I had the time to pursue my long time interest in world religions and I perused many good books on the subject – using the local library and buying many others. In particular, I was fascinated with religious thought and writings well beyond the classical main-stream religions. I was always fascinated with the life and works of Edgar Cayce who I think is the greatest seer & mystic the United States has ever known. He founded a non-denominational religious group known as the Association for Research and Enlightenment (ARE) located in Virginia Beach, Virginia – of which I have been a member for some 30-years. Cayce had the ability to go into trance and he obtained cures for many intractable illnesses, provided information on prior lives of individuals as well as little known facts about historical religious personalities. He insisted he was only reading the "Akashic Record" of individuals and events. The Akashic Record is known otherwise as the "Book of Life" which is a fascinating subject and scientists are now acknowledging that this is some kind of a holographic field of intelligence that affects the entire universe. Now that I have post-retirement time, this is my current investigative effort. Cayce was a very devoted Christian and read the bible from cover to cover each year of his life and his view of religion tracks that of the classical Christian Churches but with a better understanding of the spiritual/physical interface.

My current wife is a cradle Catholic and very devoted to her religious heritage and she is a strong advocate of Christ's admonition to "love your neighbor as yourself" and has many friends of many religious persuasions. After many years of soul-searching, I joined the Catholic Church as well and enjoy the spiritual comradeship of a large, dedicated congregation – peace at last, but my search continues for the compatible truths between science and religion.

Chapter 11 – In Retrospect

"I have promises to keep before I sleep……"

As I stated in the introduction to this book, "Surely God had plans for me". When you are a youngster, you are soley dependent upon adults for care and feeding. What you will accomplish in your life is not even on your radar screen. Living with my Uncle K.K. on their Montana ranch I mused about becoming a cowboy, thanks to the Zane Grey books I read constantly. Then as I began learning about farming in our one-room schoolhouse which included the importance of crop rotation, different breeds of animals and plant/seed selection I thought about becoming a new generation farmer. It never occurred to me that the whole farming community was in survival mode and fancy book-learning would not cut it.

Then I was saved by the bell, moved on to the big city of Bemidji, Minnesota and had other dreams. I was fascinated with science and mathematics which peaked my interest in electronics and engineering. Consequently, I spent a lot of time at the city library perusing information on the subject including ham radio and various electrical engineering projects in development. I even attended some free evening classes sponsored by the U.S. Government on electronic theory.

Soon, decisions were made for me by the outbreak of WWII and my stint in the U.S. Navy resulted in wonderful training in electronic theory as well a practical application as an electronic radar technician. This set the stage for post-war college and a degree in electrical engineering. So, my life's future work was now much clearer to me now.

But that wasn't all that life would be about and I was soon also faced with family and social obligations with demands on time, talent and finances. Of course, in the early years of adulthood I felt invincible and planning for the future was just for old people. Consequently, it was cash-in and cash-out with material desires satisfied by good income and good credit. I moved my family about six times to newer and more luxurious homes, bought nice automobiles and even an airplane or two. No worries about employment since job opportunities seemed endless. Finally, if we attended church somewhat regularly all would be well from a spiritual standpoint.

Reality began to set in as I approached fifty years of age, Drew was in college, my employment fizzled temporarily and divorce reared its ugly head. Now I became more of a realist and when my long-time employer sold the company I began to seriously plan for the future.

As I reviewed my life, both past and present, I realized I had a specific role and responsibility in life. Did I provide value-added for my family, friends, employees and God? With good intentions and some success I think I deserve a passing grade – history & legacy will eventually tell.

For my grandchildren, young nephews and nieces as well as many young cousins, I leave you with some advice from someone who has been there, done that – "Keep positive thoughts, be dependable at home and at work and remember, you are a spiritual being in a physical body – keep Christ's commandments."

I always tried to treat employees and colleagues with honesty and respect, never forgetting that they are the most important assets in a company. It has always been a pet-peeve of mine that accountants list only inanimate objects as worthwhile assets on the balance sheet while employees were hired & fired at will and could be easily replaced. I even came up with an accounting procedure that listed the cumulative employee staff as an asset based upon education, experience and importance to the company. The employee asset could be depreciated proportional to remaining working life of each employee. Alas, bankers and investors could care less.

With a new loving and caring extended family, I realized how important they were to my quality of life and I tried to provide a safety net for them within my means. They also reminded me that there is an important spiritual aspect to life. From my life-long investigation of religion's role in our life I became fixated on the fact that we are spiritual entities residing in material bodies. But which came first? The chicken or the egg? It became obvious that the Eastern Religions had it right, the spiritual entity has been created in eternity and each material life is an opportunity to provide some "value added" to the physical world around us. Although this material life is not without strife and strain, how we handle it is the key to all.

Jesus had a succinct way of expressing how you should live your life with the following admonitions:

? Love your neighbor as yourself.
? As you think so are you.

In other words, be charitable to your neighbor and watch your thoughts – they become words, watch your words-they become actions, watch your actions-they become habits, watch your habits-they become your character. If we can do this – which is hard –life will be meaningful now and forever.

I still have "Promises to keep before I sleep" to quote Robert Frost whose poetry was made famous by President Kennedy at his inauguration. Promises to my family, promises to my neighbors and most importantly promises to God.

Printed in the United States
87564LV00003B/96/A

9 781601 451620